Plough Quarterly

BREAKING GROUND FOR A RENEWED WORLD

Summer 2014, Number 1

Artists: Henry Ossawa Tanner, Nancy McKernan, Käthe Kollwitz, Walter Mason, Ghislaine Howard, Pieter Brueghel the Younger, Maria Weiss, Don Peters, Hannah Marsden, Jason Landsel. Cover: Clare Stober.

WWW.PLOUGH.COM

Plough Quarterly

BREAKING GROUND FOR A RENEWED WORLD

www.plough.com

Newly re-launching with this issue, *Plough Quarterly* features original stories, ideas, and culture to inspire everyday faith and action. Starting from the conviction that the teachings and example of Jesus can transform and renew our world, it aims to apply them to all aspects of life, seeking common ground with all people of goodwill regardless of creed. The goal of *Plough Quarterly* is to build a living network of readers, contributors, and practitioners so that, in the words of Hebrews, we may "spur one another on toward love and good deeds."

Plough Quarterly is a publication of Plough, the publishing house of the Bruderhof. The Bruderhof is an international movement of Christian communities whose members are called to follow Jesus together in the spirit of the Sermon on the Mount and of the first church in Jerusalem, sharing all our talents, income, and possessions (Acts 2 and 4). Bruderhof communities, which include both families and single people from a wide range of backgrounds, are located in the United States, England, Germany, Australia, and Paraguay. Visitors are welcome at any time. To learn more about the Bruderhof's faith, history, and daily life, or to find a Bruderhof community near you to arrange a visit, go to *www.bruderhof.com*.

Editors: Peter Mommsen, Sam Hine, Maureen Swinger. Art director: Emily Alexander.
Web editor: Carole Vanderhoof. Contributing editors: Charles Moore, Matina Horning, Chris Voll.

Founding Editor: Eberhard Arnold (1883–1935)

Plough Quarterly No. 1: Living the Sermon on the Mount
Published by Plough Publishing House, ISBN 978-0-87486-591-2
Copyright © 2014 by Plough Publishing House. All rights reserved.
Back-cover art: Egon Schiele, *Krumau – Crescent of Houses* (public domain).

Editorial Office	*Subscriber Services*	*United Kingdom*	*Australia*
151 Bowne Drive	P.O. Box 345	Brightling Road	4188 Gwydir Highway
Walden, NY 12586	Congers, NY 10920-0345	Robertsbridge	Elsmore, NSW
T: 845.572.3455	T: 800.521.8011	TN32 5DR	2360 Australia
info@plough.com	*subscriptions@plough.com*	T: +44(0)1580.883.344	T: +61(0)2.6723.2213

Plough Quarterly (ISSN 2372-2584) is published quarterly by Plough Publishing House, 151 Bowne Drive, Walden, NY 12586.
Individual subscription $32 per year in U.S.; Canada add $8, other countries add $16.
Application to mail at periodicals postage pricing is pending at Walden, NY and additional mailing offices.
POSTMASTER: Send address changes to *Plough Quarterly*, P.O. Box 345, Congers, NY 10920-0345.

Dear Reader,

How close do we dare to get to the Sermon on the Mount?

The scene is a Galilean hill thronged with people. "When Jesus saw the crowds, he went up the mountain; and after he sat down, his disciples came to him. Then he began to speak, and taught them. . . ."

So begins the biblical report of the extraordinary manifesto now known as the Sermon on the Mount (Matt. 5–7). It's widely considered the key to understanding who Jesus was and what mission he strove to fulfill. For two millennia, countless people have wrestled to apply it, from Augustine to Luther to Tolstoy to Gandhi.

Alongside much wisdom, there has been much evasion, prompting Jewish theologian Pinchas Lapide's tart comment: "The history of the impact of the Sermon on the Mount can largely be described in terms of an attempt to domesticate everything in it that is shocking, demanding, and uncompromising, and render it harmless."

There's good reason for this: Jesus' teaching is deeply disruptive, as Eberhard Arnold makes clear (page 10). It demands a top-to-bottom reordering of life, work, and social relations – that's what "repentance" means – starting with radical economic sharing, nonresistance and love of enemies, lifelong marriage between one man and one woman, and unconditional forgiveness. Remarkably, Jesus seems to really expect his followers to put his words into practice.

In this issue, we focus on people willing to get their hands dirty living out the Sermon on the Mount. Their ranks include Dorothy Day, Dietrich Bonhoeffer, John Wesley, Henri Nouwen, Mother Teresa, and others you'll meet in the following pages. Their insights are not to be consumed passively. Rather, they should inspire and equip each of us to roll up our sleeves and get to work as "doers of the word, and not merely hearers who deceive themselves."

One other note: We're thrilled that with the release of this issue, Plough's magazine is back. Founded in 1920 in Germany, Plough – which also publishes books and online content – has a history full of dramatic plot turns (see page 68). After a twelve-year hiatus, we are re-launching the magazine as a quarterly, with upcoming issues focusing on justice, children, community, peacemaking, and more.

We cordially invite you to subscribe (if you haven't already), and to urge others to do the same. Visit *www.plough.com* to read our new books, old classics, and recent articles. And please keep the responses coming – we're on this adventure together.

Warm greetings,

Peter

Peter Mommsen, Editor

Thanks to Scot McKnight for the reference to Pinchas Lapide's remarks.

Anton Mark

Kibbutz Mishol, Upper Nazareth, Israel

The World's Tallest Kibbutz

Our friends at Kibbutz Mishol live in the largest urban kibbutz in Israel. At eight stories, it's also the tallest. Established fifteen years ago, Mishol is a community of educators in Upper Nazareth. Sharing their income fully, the community's eighty adults and fifty children live together in a single building. The neighborhood is a deprived one in the country's northern periphery.

A decade ago, some commentators announced the end of the kibbutz movement. Since then, new kibbutzim like Mishol are proving them wrong. Stemming from the socialist-Zionist youth movement Hamahanot Ha'olim, whose aim is to "build a just, egalitarian society that lives in peace with its neighbors," the community has a rich cultural life, choosing to celebrate weekly, yearly, and life-cycle events together. Community practices include decision-making by consensus, communal study, and a car pool.

Where Kibbutz Mishol comes into its own, however, is through the community development work carried out by its members, including through its non-profit, Tikkun. These projects range from mentoring neighborhood children and youth to housing and supporting African refugees as they begin life in Israel.
www.tikkun.org.il

The Sanimal community, South Korea. The inscription on the pillar reads: "If you want to be my followers, you must serve one another."

A Village on the Mountain

Nestled in the mountains two hours to the southeast of Seoul is the small community

of Sanimal, which translates to "Village on the Mountain." The community of thirty-five people is a combination of families and singles who have left the consumer society of South Korea to live a life dedicated to Jesus and his way. Community life in Sanimal began in 2004, although it grew out of the larger Jsari Catholic renewal movement in the diocese of Seoul. Members bring all their possessions to contribute to the building up of God's kingdom as a reality here on earth. They support themselves through organic farming.   www.sanimal.org

Rediscovering a Hero of the Intellectual Resistance

Do you know Dietrich von Hildebrand? The SS called him "the architect of the intellectual resistance" to National Socialism in Vienna, and Pope John Paul II called him "one of the great ethicists of the twentieth century."

An ardent Christian convert, Hildebrand with his unique philosophical voice and compelling personal witness has led generations of students to a fuller and deeper relationship with the God of truth and beauty.

Our friends at the Hildebrand Project are bringing his legacy to contemporary readers

Aaron Paul

The Nurturing Community Project's 2013 gathering at the Platte Clove Bruderhof, New York.

with a number of new publications this fall, including new editions of his fundamental philosophical works, *Ethics* and *What is Philosophy?*, along with classics such as *Purity and Virginity* and *Liturgy and Personality*. And in collaboration with Image Books, they will be releasing the first English translation of Hildebrand's anti-Nazi papers, *He Dared Speak the Truth*.

www.hildebrandlegacy.org

A New Crop of Christian Communities

In many cities from San Diego to Brooklyn, from Vancouver to Orlando, a new generation of Christian intentional communities is springing to life. Sometimes called the New Monasticism, this movement has now been going for at least a decade. How can these communities encourage and help one another grow in their Christ-centered life together? The Nurturing Communities Project (NCP) seeks to fill this need by bringing together both newer and more established groups for learning and inspiration. On the NCP's behalf, David Janzen, a four-decade veteran of communal living from Reba Place Fellowship, has visited scores of newer communities. He explains: "Christian community is a new yet ancient calling. Our project is about sharing wisdom and building a network of mutual support."

One fruit of this intergenerational work is Janzen's book *The Intentional Christian Community Handbook* (Paraclete, 2012). A few more established communities have offered financial support to the NCP and have taken turns hosting its annual gathering, including last year's at the Platte Clove Bruderhof. The 2014 gathering will take place at Reba Place Fellowship in Evanston, Illinois on October 10–13. www.shalommissioncommunities.org

Ending Hunger through Self-Reliance

Matilda Aba Tibuah was born in Ekurobadze community, part of The Hunger Project's Taido Epicenter in Ghana. As a small farmer, she was unable to earn enough income for her family due to poor yields. After completing a Hunger Project workshop as well as participating in food security trainings and a microfinance program, Matilda now supports her four children with income from two acres of maize and cassava and a small shop she started.

Matilda is one of many Hunger Project partners in fifteen thousand villages across Africa, South Asia, and Latin America. Her story depicts the Hunger Project's vision of a world where every woman, man, and child leads a healthy, fulfilling life of self-reliance and dignity. Established in 1977, its approach is built upon the creativity and strength of people and communities who are leading their own change.
www.thp.org

Matilda Aba Tibuah, Ghana: "The Hunger Project brought some confidence into my life that I can do better than I am doing now."

The Hunger Project

The Best of Classic
Children's Bibles

Do you remember your first Bible?

I do – especially the picture of Daniel in the lion's den.

Those hungry lion eyes make an impression on a three-year-old. So does the angel at Daniel's shoulder, keeping back the great beasts. In later life, I've often sensed that such an angel could be there for me in times of danger.

An illustrated Bible can be a wonderful way to introduce scripture to a child, but it can be challenging to find one that portrays the glorious drama of God's history with reverence and realism. Here are some classics.

The original edition of *The Bible in Pictures for Little Eyes* has vibrant paintings that many children find unforgettable. The text is geared to two- and three-year-olds, sometimes too much so. (Jesus turns the water into grape juice? The temple is called a church?) My dad solved the problem by paraphrasing while we looked at the pictures. Now my husband and I take the same approach with our children.

In our early school years, my siblings and I loved *Egermeier's Bible Storybook.* The stories are written in a simple yet powerful style, with pictures on many but not all pages. (They could have at least shown us Jonah and the whale!) Still, the illustrations drew us in. Children often latch onto a certain face when they think of Jesus – I responded to the strength and compassion in these portraits of God's son as a carpenter.

From William Hole, *The Life of Jesus of Nazareth*

Older school-age children love the *Golden Children's Bible,* with text based closely on the biblical original. On each page there are vivid, dramatic pictures or maps – the stories of Moses and the prophets stand out. One criticism: Jesus is not represented as a man of his place and time – he's blond and blue-eyed. This lapse did give us an opening to talk with our children about how no one truly knows how Jesus looked. Far more important is what he said, did, and asked us to do.

Our own children's favorite Bible is a time-worn volume passed down to them from their great-grandmother. Published in 1906, *The Life of Jesus of Nazareth* has eighty paintings by the Scottish painter William Hole, with text taken from the King James version. It's out of print, but well worth tracking down.

The painter spent years in the Holy Land in a quest to capture the spirit of Jesus' land and people, and the result is powerful and haunting. Our six-year-old daughter will sit gazing at the pages for hours. When I saw her studying the crucifixion scenes, my first impulse was to take the book away until she was older. I didn't, and watching her as she looked, I felt sorrow for Jesus' cruel death in a new way. She wasn't traumatized. Afterward, she and I had better discussions about Good Friday – about suffering and compassion and new life – than after any other Bible story time. *Maureen Swinger*

The Bible in Pictures for Little Eyes, Kenneth N. Taylor, (Moody, 1978). *Egermeier's Bible Story Book,* Egermeier, Hall and Uptton (Warner Press, 2008). *The Golden Children's Bible* (Golden Books, 2006). *The Life of Jesus of Nazareth: Eighty Pictures,* William Hole (Eyre & Spottiswoode, 1906).

Purity in a Porn Age

STEVE CLIFFORD

I love my city, London, and I am proud to live in it. I love its energy, its creativity, and its glorious multitude of cultures.

But there is much which distresses me about London: the extremes of wealth, the obsession with "stuff," and the sexually saturated atmosphere. My journeys on the London Tube bring me face to face with ads featuring attractive women dressed with little left to the imagination, as well as offers to sort out any erectile dysfunction. *My Metro,* a free newspaper, offers me "personal services." The phone app Tinder invites me to "hook up" with any available woman within a five-kilometer radius.

That's just London, you might say. Yet even your teenager, safe in his or her bedroom "doing homework," has London and worse just one click, swipe, or tap away. According to the Porn Scars initiative, one third of ten-year-olds have viewed pornography online, while the largest group of internet porn viewers consists of children age twelve to seventeen. Sex has become an industry in which people are translated into a commodity to be bought and sold, or, slightly more subtly, to be used to sell products.

Against this backdrop, how does the two-thousand-year-old teaching of Jesus apply now? He told his Jewish audience: "You have heard that it was said, 'You shall not commit adultery'" (Matt. 5:27–30). But he doesn't leave it with a prohibition of an external act. He raises the bar: "But I tell you, anyone who looks at a woman lustfully has already committed adultery with her in his heart."

Right actions are not enough; what is going on in the head matters equally. Sexual sin starts in our minds when we treat someone made in God's image as an object of gratification. Jesus will not allow such a dehumanizing process, in which real people – a stranger on the bus, a colleague at work, or a member of our church – are used to feed our sexual appetite. Whether it's looking the wrong way or dwelling on inappropriate options, it falls into the head space called lust.

So what can we do? To some of us, Jesus' teaching may seem impossible. Perhaps we can start by recognizing our profound need of God's help. Then, relying on his abundance of grace, we can take a few practical steps:

- Let's ask God to help us to see people as individuals made in the image of God, refusing to allow them to become "things."
- Let's avoid those particular situations which we know make us vulnerable.
- Let's regard that unwelcome thought, that doorway to lust, as an enemy rather than a friend. A quick prayer in Jesus' name will often see it go.
- Finally, let's keep accountable. Have someone in your life whom you will tell about your own struggles, however embarrassing it might feel. Bringing these issues to the light breaks their power, because light and darkness cannot coexist.

The amazing truth that Scripture reveals to us is that God understands. Jesus was tempted in every way we are, yet without sinning (Heb. 4:15–16). He doesn't leave us on our own, but promises to be with us through his Holy Spirit. We can learn to lean into him and find strength to make the right decision.

However bad our past missteps or our present struggles and sins, forgiveness is available. We don't have to live with our guilt. Jesus comes to us, forgiving us and equipping us for everything we face, no matter where we live. Even in London. ⇝

Steve Clifford is general director of the Evangelical Alliance, United Kingdom.

CHRIS VOLL

Nancy McKernan, *Newstead Creek*, watercolor, 2003

Fighting Drought with Trees

According to a Chinese proverb, the best time to plant a tree was twenty years ago, and the next best time is now. Here at the Danthonia Bruderhof, we're working to make up for lost time. Since 2007, we've planted upwards of fifty thousand trees across 160 hectares of our New South Wales farm.

Recent weather cycles haven't been supportive. We started six years into Australia's "millennium drought" (2001 to 2009), planting a mix of native and exotic species – eucalypts, she-oaks, tea trees, common alder, nettle tree, red and white ash – in wind-breaking beltways twenty-five meters wide looping along ridge tops. When no rain came, we watered what trees we could, and watched others die. There followed two wet years when farms and towns in our area battled floods, and then since early 2012 we've been sliding back into drought. Despite our best efforts, we've lost about a third of the trees we've planted. Still, we replant, tend, and water – and accept the truth that only God can make a tree grow.

After all, this is the Australian bush, touted by its oft-quoted poet Dorothea Mackellar as a land "of droughts and flooding rains." *Caveat agricola* – farm at your own risk. Around here, you can do the math on your fingers: in a ten-year span, expect two bumper years, three average, and five subpar to poor years. That's if

Chris Voll lives in Elsmore, New South Wales, Australia.

all goes well. Like most farms in the Australian bush, ours has endured generations of sheep and cattle chomping vegetation down to the roots and trampling the frangible soil into dusty moonscapes. The old-timers will tell you they had no choice. You farmed with one eye on the weather and the other on the bank, made your money when the rain came, and flogged the land when it didn't – nothing that a crop-duster and a load of superphosphates couldn't fix up.

The result has been rapid and widespread decline in soil health as erosion, salinization, acidification, and other maladies exact a heavy toll in lost agricultural productivity and revenue.[1] The process began less than two hundred years ago, when European settlers began clearing the land and brought in non-native livestock. A 2010 report by Australia's national science agency concluded that the soil organic carbon stocks on agricultural land is forty to sixty percent lower than when the land was cleared.[2] That degradation could be as high as eighty percent, according to Dr. Christine Jones, founder of the Australian Soil Carbon Accreditation Scheme.

That's why for us at Danthonia, planting trees isn't just about beautifying our land; it's about ensuring that there will be land worth passing on to the next generation, land healthy enough to withstand the vagaries of an unforgiving and ever-changing climate. While there's no such thing as drought-proof farming, there are field-tested ways to better the odds. Planting trees is one of them – and of course, soil is where it starts.

Some may see preserving soil carbon as a noble ecological cause or a profitable business move, but for us it's more basic: more soil carbon equals more water retention. For a hectare of land with a soil depth of thirty centimeters, increasing carbon levels by just one percent enables the soil to retain an added 160,000 liters of water.[3] In an eight-year drought, that can

determine whether a farm survives.

Trees improve soil carbon by contributing organic matter throughout their lifecycle, as roots, leaves, bark, flowers, and fruit grow and then die and rot. But their real importance comes from the microclimate they help create. Already the trees we planted seven years ago stand higher than a man. The shaded grass around them is lush, and the paddocks on the leeward side of the plantings look healthier, proving the rule that a pasture's fertility is improved to a distance four times the height of the trees. Since grasses are the champions in soil-carbon production, a virtuous cycle is beginning, with healthier soil retaining more water and so supporting more biomass, which in turn will add even more soil carbon.

There are other benefits too. The tree beltways are wildlife corridors that swarm with insects and birds. In four years of recordkeeping, we've marked a twenty-seven percent surge in bird species sighted.

Trees may save our land – at least if everything works as we hope. No doubt the Australian climate still has a few surprises in store for us. In the meantime, our trees teach us to take the long view, to willingly sweat for the benefit of children yet to be born, to celebrate incremental victories, to mark the miracle that is all growing things. We plant them, tend them, and trust they are harbingers of better days to come. ⌁

1. Jonathan Sanderman, Ryan Farquharson, and Jeffrey Baldock, *Soil Carbon Sequestration Potential: A review for Australian agriculture,* CSIRO Land and Water, 2010.

2. The value of lost agricultural production due to soil acidification alone has been estimated at $ 1.6 billion AUD per year. State of the Environment 2011 Committee, *Australia State of the Environment 2011,* Australian Government Department of Environment, 2011.

3. Our neighbor Glenn compiled recent studies in Glenn David Morris, "Sustaining National Water Supplies by Understanding the Dynamic Capacity that Humus Has to Increase Soil Water," thesis submitted for Master of Sustainable Agriculture, University of Sydney, July 2004.

The Jesus
of the Four Gospels

EBERHARD ARNOLD

One thing is clear to us: as the church, we must hold to Jesus.
Everything depends on this, that we place the Jesus of the four Gospels, the son of Mary, the man who was executed under Pontius Pilate, in the center of our faith and our life, and keep to him. This Jesus has become unknown. His words have been distorted and disfigured, his work weakened. All the more, we must rediscover this Jesus and hold him up before all the world.

Our life together in the church must be oriented by nothing else but by Jesus' life, his word, and his working. Our commission is to bear the love of Christ, which is poured into our hearts by the Holy Spirit. This love, free of the unclarity of human thinking and feeling, was manifested perfectly and unmistakably in the life Jesus lived. Through Jesus' death and resurrection, his life was sealed as the revelation of God's heart. The Holy Spirit, *John 6:27* when it descended on the first church in Jerusalem, made this sealing of *Acts 2* Jesus' life known to the church so that it might follow Jesus and carry his life back into the world.

Jesus prophesied that the Spirit would remind the church of everything he had said. Within the church the Spirit will put Jesus' life into the clearest light, revealing through it the entire future of the kingdom of God. Further, the Spirit, through the active mission of the church, will convict and convince the world in regard to sin, righteousness, and judgment. . . . *John 16:7–11* The prince of this world, the spirit of the age that rules everywhere over *Luke 10:18* all peoples, is judged by Jesus – judged not by legions of angel princes *Matt. 26:53* answering Satan's violence with violence, but by the perfect love of Jesus Christ, revealed on the cross. . . .

In his living and in his dying, Jesus disclosed the goodness and love of God's heart in a way unique in time and space. Whoever steps forward to stand by his side and is gripped by this total love is free from the judgment pronounced on the spirit of this world and age. Of course, any who want to follow the prince of this world – the zeitgeist that controls people and governs the earth as its god – are subject to the same judgment

---

Eberhard Arnold delivered the sermon from which this article is excerpted on May 13, 1934 at the Rhön Bruderhof, a Christian community near Fulda, Germany. This community, which had been raided by the Gestapo shortly after Hitler's rise to power a year before, was being increasingly targeted by the National Socialist regime; Arnold's reference to a "murderous" zeitgeist reflects this context. (In 1937, the community would in fact be dissolved "for political reasons.") For more from Arnold, see Salt and Light: Living the Sermon on the Mount *(Plough, 1998).*

pronounced on him, since they follow the injustice of his mammon, the falsehood and lying and unfaithfulness of his deceit, and the murderous impulses of the abyss.

By contrast, those who follow and believe in Jesus have forsaken the destructive fury of the devil and his works. They are not judged, for they have already been judged: they have experienced the judgment of the spirit of the church, which has been carried out and is continually being carried out on their hearts, lives, and old human identity. They are judged in the new sense, that of grace, through which the spirit of Jesus Christ gives itself to them and renews them completely in the very act of judgment.

After his baptism by John and temptation in the wilderness, Jesus began

his ministry by proclaiming the good news: "The kingdom of God has *Matt. 4:17* drawn near!" Yet he prefaced this good news with a call for his hearers to repent: to change their whole way of thinking, to overthrow completely their entire previous lives.

Jesus' message is: Change your lives radically in every way – prepare for the coming kingdom by turning upside down everything you have up till now felt, thought, and done. The supreme event is imminent, compared *Mark 1:15* to which all other events in human history are insignificant. Now God is *John 1:14* coming to us. Now history is really starting. True, there has been preparatory history, but now the real history is beginning, the history that will decide, interrupt, and transform everything. For the kingdom of God is coming. Get ready for it.

This is what matters now: Love God! Change so much that you will *Matt. 22:37* be able to love with your whole hearts. Change your lives so that everything you do will be nothing but love to him. Change in such a way that this love to God will be not just a personal matter of your hearts but will mean for you the revolution of all things, the abolition of all injustice, and the conquest of all countries and all peoples for God's reign. Until now *1 Peter 5:8* you have been under the sway of the beast of prey that prowls around *2 Cor. 11:13–15* you, disguised as an angel of light and persuading you to set your hope on gradual progress. Therefore you must change your thinking completely, so that you cannot succumb to the beast's seductive influence. Believe only in this one joyful message: God is near! His sovereignty is breaking in! You can expect good from no other source. Your thinking must be trans- *Rom. 12:2* formed, your life must take a new direction. Believe in this message, this news, this evangel!

In his talk with Nicodemus at the beginning of the Gospel of John, Jesus says that we will only be able to recognize this kingdom and be incorporated into it if we completely restart our life. When a baby is born, a completely new being arrives in our midst. As yet we know nothing about the child except that it is here and is starting its life. This is exactly the way it should be for anyone who wants to see and enter the kingdom of God. An individual must be renewed to such an extent that he or she becomes as a newborn child, starting life fresh from the very beginning.

John 3:1–10

This rebirth, however, takes place in a very definite context. Just as a child is born into a family, so a person who is reborn through the Spirit is born into the kingdom. The surroundings into which such a one is born, the vista that he or she sees from the hour of this new birth, is God's kingdom and nothing but God's kingdom. So do not be surprised that you have to be born again – otherwise you could never see the kingdom. And bear in mind that what matters about your personal rebirth is not your own experience but the kingdom of God. That which seems most subjective is in fact the most objective.

James 1:18

We find the clearest picture of this mysterious rebirth – this birth into a new world – near the beginning of the Gospel of Matthew, in the Sermon of the Mount. This Sermon shows us the nature and character of the new reborn life of the kingdom of God. It shows us what landscape one sees, what kind of world one is born into, once one is truly reborn.

Matt. 5–7

The new life of rebirth brings a justice that cannot be compared with any human morality, social order, or theology – a justice that is nothing but the goodness of God's heart. This new justice is better than anything ever thought, felt, willed, or spoken by humans, for it is God's own doing.

The new justice is the outpouring of God's spirit, the essence of his innermost life. It is God's nature, his substance, his basic working – and thus it is life at its most vibrant, movement and activity at their most free. This new righteousness is a life born of God, and for this reason it is utterly opposed to every kind of self-righteousness or human justice. These both stem from consciousness of self and of one's own rightful claims. But divine justice – the new righteousness – begins by becoming a beggar, by becoming poor and being judged, by extinguishing all claims to possessions, rights, and privileges.

Mark 10:41–45

What is more, the new justice begins under the weight of the whole world's suffering. It begins at the point where the whole world's load of pain presses down on a believing human heart. To be sure, human justice knows something of compassion for suffering too, but it quickly reverts to a bloodthirsty hatred against those who caused the suffering. Human justice thus turns into injustice, since from among the guilty – and in fact all are guilty – it seeks out a group of particularly guilty people on whom to avenge itself.

In the midst of this absence of love or peace, the justice of the new kingdom of Jesus Christ seeks the all-embracing peace of God. It desires

Mark 2:17   the kindliness that has a heart for all people, including the guiltiest, and is merciful even to those who have sinned most gravely against peace and justice. This new justice is revealed as God's heart – a heart ready to sacrifice and ready to die, which does not want to kill the guilty but rather to be killed for them, so that they may become innocent by grasping the meaning and value of this sacrifice: the readiness of the heart of God to

John 12:32   offer itself up, even to the last drop of blood. God can be found only if we are prepared to suffer death – including sacrifice of the physical body, which we cling to as our last entitlement and prerogative – for the sake of his righteousness and his kingdom. Only then are we truly reborn for the kingdom of God.

In the first verses of the Sermon on the Mount, Jesus thus opens a way for us to understand the kingdom of God. From this starting point, the rest of the Sermon follows naturally.

Now you must love your enemies. For love's sake you will surrender your

Matt. 5:39–40   last possessions, down to the last coat and the last shirt. Now you will not pay back force with force. You will not resist evil by responding with evil.

Here you will find faithfulness, and in faithfulness, purity in both

Matt. 5:27–30   physical and emotional relationships. You will find the truly better righteousness manifested as perfect love and as eternal loyalty in love – and therefore also as the inviolability of monogamous marriage.

Matt. 5:48   You shall in your way be perfect, just as the Father himself is perfect. In your words you are to be perfect too, saying nothing superfluous but

Matt. 5:33–37   speaking the truth simply, clearly, and to the point. There is no other truthfulness than that of love; there is no other perfection than that of love.

Can you not see what thwarts and destroys love? It is mammon. You

Matt. 6:24   cannot serve both God and mammon; you cannot serve both ownership and love, nor both material worries and trusting love. Whoever heaps up possessions – whoever holds on to even the least private property for his own interest while his brothers and sisters are hungry and cold and lack a roof over their heads – has no love. Because of this, Jesus says, do not gather property. Have nothing at all belonging to yourselves; have no hidden treasures or reserves anywhere.

Matt. 6:19–20

But do not worry about your livelihood either. Those who are fearful about necessities seek just as anxiously to preserve the material basis for life as those who cling to their bank account or real estate. All this belongs to mammon just as much as hanging on to property does. The gray fog of worry stems from mammon just as surely as the golden glitter of money. Therefore do not worry. Learn from nature, which you should love because it is God's creation. Look at the birds and flowers. Believe in the loving Father, who sets their table for them and gives them their feathers and colorful raiment.

Matt. 6:25–34

The righteousness of the kingdom of God, the renewal of the reborn heart, means singleness of heart. The heart can be compared to an inner eye which is focused on God alone. If your inner eye is really concentrated on God, you cannot have a fortune, nor can you have any worries either. Instead you will grasp that to call upon God is to trust in his love. To pray is to plead for God's dominion. It is to do his will and hallow his name. It is the gift of daily bread, spiritual as well as temporal. With this clear inner eye, you will have new, loving hearts, free from evil and the rule of violence, free from the temptation and trials that will shake this world right up to its last hour. In *this* way call upon God.

Matt. 6:22

Matt. 6:5–13

This love to God means love to all people, for God loves all and his heart is directed toward all. He is merciful to all and lets his sun shine on all and gives his rain to all. A person who through the love of God has experienced new birth cannot judge anyone else; we must have faith for everyone. Jesus tells us: Do not judge others; love them. Judgment means passing a final, conclusive verdict. This you must never do. Love's hope and faith's trust must always leave open the way to return home, to be saved for God's kingdom.

Matt. 5:45

Matt. 7:1

Nevertheless, for the sake of the love you have for God, beware of surrendering what is holiest in your heart to those who are not ready for it. For then you would be abandoning true love to God in favor of a sham love. Speak to people as befits their inner receptiveness, in a way they can grasp, but do so without denying the least grain of the truth. Either of these would be a sin against love for God – to judge others, or to share indiscriminately what is holy with people who are not yet awakened. . . .

Matt. 7:6

Matt. 7:12   Deal with all people as you wish them to act toward you. You wish for yourselves that God may care for you in body, soul, and mind. What you expect for yourselves you should make possible for everyone. And this

Matt. 5:46–48   should be done without exceptions. This is the new justice. You must not limit the good works of your love to people congenial to you, for God loves all people, no matter what they are like. Therefore you, too, must love all people with God's love, and do to them everything that you wish done to you and yours. The genuine love, the new justice that is for *all* – this is the truth of God's kingdom.

The narrow gate through which you must enter is summed up in this

Matt. 7:13–14   evangelical counsel: Treat every person just as you would like to be treated yourselves, and as you would like your dearest family members to be treated. This new justice is better than that of all the moralists and theologians. It is the narrow mountain path, the entry into the kingdom of

Matt. 5:14   God, the ascent to the city on the hill. Love others as you love yourselves. Do this because you love God and because you have experienced that God loves each person. You take for granted that your own body, soul, and mind need caring for – so make it your business to care for everyone else's in the same way. Only then will you find the door to God's kingdom,

Matt. 7:21–23   following the narrow path that leads along the precipice upward to his city.

At first there will be very few of you who go this way. Troublesome spirits and hostile powers will oppose you. Their outward violence will be able to do little harm to you, for it cannot kill your conscience or change

Matt. 7:15–20   your will. More dangerous is false prophecy, which joins forces with this violence and tries to confuse the single eye. Therefore it is necessary for you to learn to recognize false prophecy. You will know it by its deeds, above all by this one identifying mark: whether it takes sides with the beast of prey or not. Everything that is connected with the beast's rapacious nature – mammon, faithless carnal passion, the shedding of blood, dishonest business profits, collective egoism[1] – is false prophecy. Beware of the veiled nature of the beast of prey that lurks in false prophecy.

Love the true prophets. You will know them by their love. This love can ultimately be recognized in that the true prophet gives his or her life

John 15:13   for the brothers and sisters. Readiness to sacrifice one's own physical life, without injuring any other life – this is the mark of true prophecy.

---

1. "Collective egoism" is a coinage by French communitarian anarchist Pierre-Joseph Proudhon (1809–1865) describing the tendency of groups to behave based on self-interest.

In the Sermon on the Mount, Jesus discloses the character of the new way of life and the new kingdom; he shows the nature of the new building of life that cannot collapse, that cannot be corrupted by any worldly power.   *Matt. 7:24–27*

Everything that Jesus said, he did as well. Everything he proclaimed in the Sermon on the Mount and in his parables he put into practice. He did so by gathering his twelve disciples into an itinerant fellowship, sharing all possessions in a common life characterized by homelessness and by dedication in love. He did so too by sending these disciples out as God's ambassadors of the coming kingdom, charged to represent the full authority and the complete love of the kingdom of God in their mission.   *Matt. 10:1–8*

Jesus proved the amazing strength and endurance of his commitment to this fellowship by remaining true to it, despite his disciples' persistent foolishness, right to the end – until they fled while he was crucified. And he proved it in the diligence with which he instructed his disciples in the truth of his teachings right up until his death.

In this way the four Gospels in the New Testament came into being. Though written long after Jesus' death, they derive from his daily practice of giving instruction and then the continuance of this practice in the church. Whenever the church gathered, stories of Jesus would be told. . . . Through this oral transmission – through the joy of telling over and over again who Jesus was and what he did and said – the truth was carried from heart to heart, from one life into another.

At the end of the Gospel of John it is reported that Jesus did many other things, but if they were all to be written down, the world could not hold the books that would have to be written. All the same, those deeds which were recorded show us clearly the content of Jesus' life in all its authority. What he did when with his circle of companions was nothing different from what he taught and proclaimed: it was an expression of a love that offers itself up equally in body, soul, and mind. His actions demonstrated the future he proclaimed.   *John 21:25*

This is most obvious in the driving out of demons and diabolical powers; as Jesus said, the kingdom of God is present when devils are driven from human bodies by the finger of the Holy Spirit. Likewise, his healings showed that death – and the root of death, sin – are done away with through Jesus' coming and the approach of God's kingdom. . . .

Death is the last weapon of the satanic power. And so Jesus turned to those who had died, bringing people back to life whose bodies were already decomposing. He touched corpses: the dead were awakened by his intervention. Precisely in regard to death he had to demonstrate the power of life. Without resurrection the gospel of God and his life is null and void. . . .

Yet Jesus' deeds were not limited to helping human beings; his work
went even further. . . . When Jesus stilled the storm that raged over the Sea of Galilee and when he made the fig tree wither, he showed that all the other elements of creation, too, must be touched by his breath and the approach of his kingdom. He showed that he reigns over all forces in creation, that everything must be transformed into something completely new.

Mark 4:35–41

Thus, everything Jesus did points toward the end of days and to the coming of God's kingdom, when the natural world of the first creation will experience one final miracle affecting human bodies as well. His deeds show that God's love is directed not only toward the souls of human beings, but just as much toward physical existence and toward the whole natural order. To be sure, what happens in each individual soul remains decisive, otherwise no person could take part in this renewal. But God's great interest is directed toward all of creation and the natural order of the whole universe, so that they may all be included in his new creation, the kingdom of God. . . . Accordingly, Jesus' authority to forgive sins will become visible through driving evil out of individual hearts – not so that they may overrate the experiences of their own small souls, but so that they can become free for the mighty work that encompasses everything: the approach of God's kingdom.

Rev. 21:1–5

This means destroying the works of the devil. The creation, spoiled by Satan's malign influence, will be restored to the fullness of life that God originally intended for it. All Jesus' deeds are a sign and a symbol of the greatness that is to come when the invincible life of the second creation will be manifest, when death, the last enemy, will be vanquished and when God, the Creator Spirit, will reign over renewed nature.

1 John 3:8

Rev. 22:1–5

Rom. 8:19–25

It was necessary for this mystery to be revealed in and through Jesus himself. That is why he truly rose from the dead. He, the Risen One, is present in the church through the pouring out of the Holy Spirit, in fulfilment of his promise: "I am with you always, till the end of the world. All authority in heaven and on earth has been given to me." Here, in the Holy

Matt. 28:18–20

18

Spirit, the King of the coming kingdom, he who conquers all worlds for God, is present in the church. The Holy Spirit, being the substance of the church's life, is the guarantor of the joyful news that Jesus is coming as king of the ultimate kingdom. ➤

John 14:15–21

Translated from Hella Römer's stenography by Nicoline Maas and Hela Ehrlich. Arnold's words have been edited for conciseness.

Who Is Eberhard Arnold?

Jürgen Moltmann

From the foreword to a forthcoming collection of Arnold's essays,
Leben im Licht, *ed. Daniel Hug (Plough, 2015).*

Eberhard Arnold's voice is as authentically prophetic and as immediately compelling as it was ninety years ago. It is the voice of a Christian just as radical as Christoph Blumhardt before him and Dietrich Bonhoeffer after him. It is a wakeup call for the religiously sedated and socially domesticated Christendom of the Western world. I read and hear it as "the voice of one crying in the wilderness" of today's world. Eberhard Arnold lived, believed, and thought in the revolutionary situation of Germany after World War I – amidst Spartacus-style uprisings by Communists, assassinations by nationalists, soaring public debt, inflation, and general confusion. As a result of this, I believe, he saw down to the root of things, leading to uncompromising decisions in the discipleship of Jesus between the old, transient world and the future of God's new world.

Especially impressive to me are his incorrigible hope in the kingdom of God and his wide-ranging love for this earth. He was no sectarian, but rather a universalist in his love for life. The Bruderhof communities which he founded serve, in the tradition of the Anabaptist communities of the Reformation period, as beacons of an alternative hope amid the lethal dangers of our time. They are not *die Stillen im Lande* ["the quiet people in the nation," a term applied to Pietists]; rather, they are children of "God's revolution," the peaceful revolution to which Eberhard Arnold dedicated himself. His message to us today is anything but innocuous – it is thoroughly unsettling, expansive, and trailblazing.

Translated by Peter Mommsen

Jürgen Moltmann, pioneer of the "theology of hope," is professor emeritus of systematic theology at Tübingen University. His students have included Miroslav Volf and Peter Zimmerling.

"I have no right to withdraw from the responsibility of being an advocate. It is my duty to voice the sufferings of people, the sufferings that never end and are as big as mountains." So wrote Käthe Kollwitz – artist, socialist, pacifist, and grieving mother – five years after her son Peter died on the battlefield in World War I. In 1937, she began working on her Pietà in his memory as war loomed again. In that second great bloodletting she would lose her grandson, also named Peter, killed in action as a draftee for Hitler, whose regime was hounding Kollwitz for her dissident activities.

In 1993, an enlarged casting of the Pietà was installed as the centerpiece of Germany's National Memorial to the Victims of War and Tyranny on Berlin's Unter den Linden boulevard. The sculpture is situated in the Neue Wache guardhouse, once a nationalistic shrine that played a central role in the Nazis' annual parade for war heroes.

Today, the remains of an unknown soldier and an unknown concentration camp prisoner rest beneath Kollwitz's statue. Directly overhead, the oculus allows sunlight, rain, and snow to fall onto the agonized mother. "Blessed are those who mourn" – this place draws us into the heart of this cryptic beatitude, evoking the suffering of mothers all over the world, from Syria to the Congo.

Berlin photographer Walter Mason writes: "Kollwitz's statue, alone in the middle of the room, commands a respect that is immediately understood by anyone who enters. The tourists come in off the street and, without exception, fall silent. The mother with her son is so wrapped up in her sorrow that she seems unapproachable; the visitors stand at a distance and partake in her grief." ➤   *The Editors*

Käthe Kollwitz, *Mother with Her Dead Son*
Photograph by Walter Mason

Ghislaine Howard, *The Seven Works of Mercy: Burying the Dead*

We Are Not Bystanders

An interview with Cardinal Donald Wuerl on discipleship and politics,
and on Pope Francis's advice to pastors (and the rest of us)

Cardinal Donald Wuerl is the Archbishop of Washington.

Plough: *Does the Sermon on the Mount apply only to those with a special vocation, or to everyone?*

Cardinal Wuerl: The Sermon on the Mount is the call to every disciple. If you are going to follow Jesus, if you are going to walk in his pathway, it tells you: "Here is how you do it; this is what is involved."

It all begins with recognizing that the kingdom of God is coming into being right now. The Beatitudes all have this dual aspect

to them: "Blessed are . . . because. . . ." We are asked to be compassionate, to be merciful, to seek righteousness and justice, etc., because the kingdom is coming to be. We can actually help realize that kingdom, even though it is only in its beginning stage.

What part of the Sermon on the Mount do you feel is most important today?

I think of Jesus' teaching about salt and light. Matthew 5 is a wonderful presentation of the way of the kingdom, but it can't just be accepted passively. We are not bystanders in realizing the kingdom; we are supposed to be active participants. Jesus says to us, "You are supposed to be salt of the earth, salt that gives flavor. You are supposed to be light; people should see through your actions that the kingdom is coming to be."

Why is the church so involved in the works of mercy, of charity, of teaching, of social justice, and of social service? It is trying to be salt and light. So while the entire Sermon on the Mount is important, for me that is one of the most exciting parts.

How does that play out practically in everyday life?

That's the question – how can we be salt and light? I think that is the emphasis of the New Evangelization. We must begin by recognizing the onslaught of secularism. I described it once as a tsunami that has washed across Western culture – actually, human culture – and taken with it the markers of identity: marriage and family, objective right and wrong, belief in God's presence and in goodness in our lives. The New Evangelization is the call for every one of us, every believer, to renew his or her faith personally – not just cognitively by reviewing what I believe in the creed, but prayerfully. In my own heart, I must effectively renew my relationship with the Lord Jesus.

That is the first step. The second is to be confident in the truth of the gospel. The words of Jesus, everything he said – these are the words of everlasting life. We need to stand confident in that truth, even in a world that tends to marginalize it.

Then the third element is to share it. If you believe in Jesus, if you love the Lord, if you try to follow his gospel, share it. That is the challenge of our age – we have been given this beautiful gift, and if we recognize it then we need to be able to share it. We are not bystanders.

What examples do you look to for inspiration?

Well, I guess I should start at the top – I think the example right now is Pope Francis. All over the world, Christians and other people see in him something wonderful. It is not some new teaching; he is saying the same thing that the church has said for two thousand years. But with

"What Francis is showing us is that it's not enough to proclaim it – you have to live it."

him, people see someone doing it. He is living the gospel in a great simplicity that is drawing people from all over the world. They look at him and say, "This is the way it should be."

I was at an ecumenical and interfaith gathering over a month ago, and Christians of different faith communities spoke as if Francis were everybody's pope. What struck me particularly was the remark from one interfaith participant: "You know, he is showing all of us religious leaders how we are supposed to live our lives."

Pope Francis is known for living without material excess, in the spirit of his namesake Saint Francis of Assisi and of Jesus' words against serving wealth.

The Holy Father keeps reminding us to think how many people on this planet are hungry or live in abject poverty – you don't have to go too far to find poverty, even here in our own United States. The Pope is saying, "Thank God for what you have. Praise the Lord for your gifts and capabilities. But now whatever you have, use it for the good of others."

There is a widespread perception that Pope Francis will change the church's teachings, for instance on marriage and sexuality. What is your reaction?

I too hear those comments – they are all over the newspapers, radio, and television. My response – and I think it is totally verifiable by listening to what the Pope is actually saying – is always that he is not changing any of the church's teachings. Listen to what he is saying! It is what the church has always said. What Francis is showing us is that it is not enough just to proclaim: you have to live it.

In the Catholic understanding, it falls to the priest or the bishop to announce the fullness of the church's teaching in all of its clarity. You recite those Beatitudes from the pulpit, and you don't water them down. But when you come out of the pulpit, you have to meet people where they are – you try to walk with them so that both of you can get closer to the Lord Jesus. I think that is what the Pope is saying. We are not all perfect; we need to encourage one another along the path. Some people unfortunately see this through their own lens and read more into it.

What should we expect from the second year of Francis's pontificate?

This first year has been a year of excitement for the world, because people are seeing the power of the gospel to attract. Going into this second year, I think we are probably going to see some of the fruit of his commitment to restructure the Curia. Remember, the Curia exists to help him carry out his ministry, and he is saying, "Isn't it time we re-look at all of that to see how well it is working?"

Pope Francis appointed you to the Vatican's Congregation for Bishops, which is responsible for advising him in the selection of new bishops. Has he spoken to you about which qualities to look for in a candidate?

I am particularly pleased that you focus on what Francis actually says! Last month [February], he met with all the members of the Congregation for Bishops and told us: "When you present someone to me who you think should be named a bishop, he has to be a pastor at heart. The task of a bishop is to be a pastor of souls. He obviously has to know the faith, but then he has to be the shepherd of a flock."

Then the Pope added this: "The five virtues of a good bishop are: he has to patient, patient, patient, and patient – and he has to have patience with those who tell him to be more patient." We can't give up on people that we are trying to bring to God; we have to just keep at it, just as Jesus did.

As Archbishop of Washington, you experience at close hand the intersection of faith and politics. In a rapidly secularizing society, what is the place of Christianity in the public square?

That is the challenge: how do you proclaim the message of Jesus so that it can be heard by people who may not be disposed to hear it? The task of the church is to teach – both with our words and with our example. Jesus is the model of that. He taught tirelessly, and he showed his disciples through his life how to take his words and live them.

Our task today is to take the gospel seriously ourselves and live it in all its beauty. Then we won't have to confront other people – what they need to see is that we are convinced ourselves. This is a quiet witness, but a witness that will begin to make an impact.

Here in the nation's capital, politics is the very fabric of the city – it eats, drinks, sleeps, breathes politics. I don't need to get involved in the politics in order to be heard announcing the truth, the right, the good, the gospel.

When you meet face to face with a politician who professes Christianity but whose politics do not match the church's teachings, what do you say to him or her?

I always have to remind both of us that my job is to be a pastor of souls. I am not going to tell people how they should vote. But I am going to tell them what the gospel challenges them to do and be. And I will call them to act according to what they themselves say they are. That, I believe, is the church's role.

You have worked with the Bruderhof, the Anabaptist community behind Plough, since the 1990s. How can we build up the unity of the church across the divisions in Christianity?

That is a very important task. Imagine how powerful our witness would be if we all proclaimed the gospel with one voice in a world that is so secular, so material. I think we must start by continually nurturing the respect we have for one another, just like the two of us are doing now by sitting together talking about what is very dear to both of us: the gospel of Jesus Christ. The closer we come together, knowing and respecting each other, the more effective our ministry will be.

I would like to say how much I appreciate the work of the Bruderhof. As you mentioned, our friendship goes back many years, rooted in what we share: a very simple, basic love of the Lord. It's a respectful relationship, even though we see things very differently – if we didn't, we wouldn't be coming from two different perspectives! But I appreciate the openness and the fraternity. One thing we can say: we both want to seek first the kingdom of God. ⤳

Interview by Peter Mommsen on April 10, 2014. A video version is posted on www.plough.com.

Pieter Brueghel the Younger, *The Works of Mercy*

Ghislaine Howard, *The Seven Works of Mercy: Giving Drink to the Thirsty*

Alarmed by Jesus

An interview with Russell Moore on strange Christianity, church discipline, and why the rise of secularism is good for the church

Russell Moore, a noted ethicist and author, is president of the Ethics & Religious Liberty Commission of the Southern Baptist Convention.

Plough: *Our culture is rapidly shedding its Christian trappings. In this situation, how does the Sermon on the Mount apply to the church today?*

Russell Moore: The Sermon on the Mount is becoming increasingly relevant, because Christianity is getting stranger and stranger in our society, at least in North America. Jesus' teachings make no rational sense to the natural person, as the Apostle Paul would put it. In a Darwinistic, naturalistic account of the universe, for instance, it seems only natural to strike back when one has been hit.

The Sermon on the Mount has to do with the kingdom of God. The church is the initial manifestation of God's kingdom in this era, pointing to what the kingdom will be like in fullness in the age to come.

Where are we in greatest danger of compromise?

In my conservative evangelical wing of the church I often tell churches that too many of us are alarmed by passages in the scripture that are meant to be comforting, and are comforted by passages that are meant to be alarming. For instance, the doctrine of election alarms a great many in my community – people are fearful of what it might mean – when in reality, it is meant to assure us that God is for us and isn't going to leave us.

On the other hand, many people treat the Sermon on the Mount as if it were only to comfort us – a list of sayings to be crocheted and put on the wall. But if we really pay attention to what Jesus is saying here, he is dismantling everything about our world and creating an entirely new one for us. If we really understand the Sermon on the Mount, our response as sinners should first be dismay followed by repentance.

I remember one time when I was preaching from the Sermon on the Mount, I found myself unwittingly putting an asterisk after one passage – "Well, obviously, it can't mean that!" It hit me that this is exactly what a Protestant liberal does with the virgin birth. I had to turn around and submit myself to what Jesus was actually saying, rather than demand that his words submit to me.

In Matthew 5, Jesus teaches the indissolubility of marriage between a man and a woman. How can Christians do a better job of testifying to God's will for sexuality and marriage?

"People treat the Sermon on the Mount as if it were only to comfort us – a list of sayings to be crocheted and put on the wall."

For the past generation or so the North American church has assumed that the broader culture shares its conception of marriage, and that all we have to do is add the gospel in order to make our marriages better. Today, however, we need to return to a New Testament model of patiently explaining the theological underpinnings of marriage and sexuality.

Marriage and sexuality are not simply about how to get along better in this life. They are icons pointing to something that is prehistorical and pre-cosmic: the union of Christ and his church. Because of this, it's critical to spend time teaching God's people how their marriages and their sexual lives point either toward or away from this central truth.

It is also necessary to fight the devil. Contemporary people tend to cringe when they hear believers speaking of the devil in a personal way, but I think we must. The devil works in two ways: either by deceiving people with the message, "The Word of God doesn't apply to you – you shall not surely die," or by accusing them: "You are too sinful – you will never be acceptable to God."

As ambassadors of reconciliation, we have to fight these lies in both directions. We must expose the devil's deceit by saying, "The sexually immoral will not inherit the kingdom of God." However, we must also attack the devil's

Love your enemies. Too many Christians turn this into a formula that is easily misunderstood. That is, they say, "The Christian must love everyone." But if we ask how such a universal love should look in the concrete, we very quickly see that it does not work – or better, it can only work if it remains a mere feeling, pure emotion, a diffuse love for humanity.

The Bible is much too realistic to talk of such misty dreams. The Bible says we are to love our neighbors and also our enemies – meaning those we really have something to do with and not some millions of people we can easily love because they are so beautifully distant from us.

Gerhard Lohfink

From *No Irrelevant Jesus*, trans. L. Maloney (Liturgical, 2014).

accusation by declaring, "The blood of Christ is able to cleanse us from any sin. Jesus offers each person reconciliation on the condition of repentance and faith." Both truths need to be spoken in a world filled with sexual brokenness.

Jesus said, "Do not store up for yourselves treasures on earth. . . . You cannot serve God and mammon." Are we in the United States, the richest country on earth, being too soft on economic injustice and materialism?

Yes. All of us, whatever our disagreements over public policy, must learn to listen to the prophets who speak about systemic economic injustice, and listen to the message of our Lord's brother James, who taught that the way we treat the poor is indicative of how we are treating Christ. That has to be constantly preached, even though it's often uncomfortable. When Jesus warns against mammon he is not just speaking about very wealthy people. In a New Testament context, the most economically

struggling North American believer of today is wealthier than the "wealthy" mentioned in Scripture.

How can we better share and bear one another's economic burdens within our church communities?

For that to happen we need to know what's going on with one another. It's impossible to bear one another's burdens if we don't know what those burdens are.

I have seen positive developments in recent years when it comes to this issue. After the economic collapse in 2008, churches stepped up to bear the economic burdens of those who were suffering. Also, many evangelical Christians have become active in adopting and fostering children, acting on their responsibilities according to James 1:27 to care for orphans and widows. The rest of the church community has worked very hard to help these families economically, understanding that this is not simply the family's issue but the entire church body's issue. More of that needs to happen within our churches.

It is often noted that the Sermon on the Mount provides instruction not just to individuals but to the church community itself. What is the role of church discipline in giving a more powerful gospel witness?

The Apostle Paul says in 1 Corinthians 5:12, "I do not judge those who are on the outside. It is those on the inside that I judge." Obviously the apostle is not speaking of moral discernment, because he does have a moral discernment about the outside culture. What he is talking about is accountability. Contemporary North American Christians often reverse the Pauline formula. We judge those who are on the outside and demand accountability from them, while tending to pay no attention to the sins that are happening on the inside, within our own congregations.

We must recognize that membership in the church points to becoming the future kings and queens of the universe. We are showcasing the kingdom of God. Accordingly, a congregation that is unwilling to discipline is a congregation that represents a false gospel. The reason we hold people accountable through church discipline is not to be punitive but to be redemptive – in the words of Jesus in Matthew 18, "to gain a brother."

You have called for a transformed evangelical engagement with politics. How can this happen without falling back into the trap of serving the agendas of the political left or right?

This can happen by working with people of good will who are our allies on specific issues. This doesn't mean we'll agree with our allies all across the board. We cannot accept any political agenda *in toto.* Our aim should be to address those issues that are central to the Scriptures: neighbor-love and justice and righteousness in the public arena. But we must do so with a healthy skepticism of political structures and leaders. Political leaders are not spiritual leaders, so we must never baptize their concerns as such.

We must recognize the good, but also the limits, of political engagement. Jesus says, "Seek first the kingdom of God and his righteousness." I agree with Nicholas Wolterstorff that righteousness is not just internal piety but justice. We seek the kingdom of God and God's justice. But it must be in that order: we're informed by the gospel and must make the kingdom of God our priority.

Many Christians are worried that their faith is being marginalized in Western countries. What's your response?

As I see it, the marginalization of Christianity in society is bad for America but good for the church. For far too long we have sought to normalize Christianity. We've wanted to say to our neighbors, "We're really just like you. We're values voters. We're a moral majority. We can add Jesus to your life and give you everything to help you be a good American citizen."

Those days are vanishing, and we are seeing a "rapture" of the nominal cultural church. Those who go to church in order to earn their God-and-country badges are vanishing away in front of our eyes. Thankfully, we are being left with more and more Christians who really believe in the strangeness of the gospel message. Now we have an opportunity for clarity – an opportunity for revival. ⮞

Interview by Peter Mommsen on March 26, 2014. An audio version is posted on www.plough.com.

Thy will be done on earth, as it is in heaven. How shall we understand these words?

As thy angels offend thee not, so may we also not offend thee. As all the holy patriarchs, all the prophets, all the apostles, all the spiritual are, as it were, God's heaven, and we in comparison of them are earth, as in them, so Father in us also.

As the church of God is heaven and his enemies are earth, so we wish well for our enemies, that they, too, may believe, and so the will of God be done as in heaven, so also in earth.

As our spirit is heaven and our flesh earth; as our spirit is renewed by believing, so may our flesh be renewed by rising again, and "the will of God be done as in heaven, so in earth."

Saint Augustine

From *Our Lord's Sermon on the Mount*, VII.6.

I CANNOT LOVE what you are, no,
what you are is indeed a mistake.
But there is in you a grace that surpasses
what you obstinately are.
Something that's yours and doesn't belong to you,
in you from the start but separate from you,
that draws towards you cautiously, afraid
of its own uncontainable splendor.

No, io non posso amare quel che sei,
quello che sei è in verità uno sbaglio.
C'è in te però una grazia che oltrepassa
quello che tu in ostinatezza sei.
Qualche cosa che è tuo e non ti appartiene,
che è in te in origine ma da te diviso,
che a te si accosta cauto, spaventato
del suo stesso incontenibile splendore.

PATRIZIA CAVALLI
Translated by Gini Alhadeff

From *My Poems Won't Change the World: Selected Poems,* ed. Gini Alhadeff (Farrar, Straus and Giroux, 2013). Used by permission. Artwork: Henri Lebasque, *Girl in Boat*

Love in a Leper Colony

JOHANN CHRISTOPH ARNOLD

A fiftieth wedding anniversary always deserves recognition, but this one was truly gold. When Damián and Maria Dávalos made their wedding vows fifty years ago, they were under no illusions. Banished to Sapucay, an isolated leper colony in the hinterlands of Paraguay, they were surrounded by crippled and disfigured fellow sufferers of the then-incurable disease. They asked each other if they would still love even when their fingers curled and their skin dried and cracked.

My father once worked as director of agriculture at Sapucay. When, retracing my family story, I returned to Sapucay more than half a century later – and decades after a cure for leprosy had been found – I was surprised to find some of the same people still living there. Though they could have returned to their homes and families, the lingering stigma in society was so strong that many chose to remain.

Today Damián and Maria laugh as they recall the first time their glances met. The joy they exude is remarkable, considering all they have suffered. In earlier years when they were healthier, medicines to treat the disease were donated to be distributed free to the patients. However, the corrupt colony administration required the patients to pay. By the time Damián and Maria were able to afford the medication it was too late; the damage to their bodies had been done.

Yet Damián and Maria are not bitter. Seeing God in the nature surrounding them and in the stars, they say, has helped them find peace, hope, and the strength to forgive. And both express thankfulness for all the friends they have made over the years. "One who has friends is alive, but one with no friends is dead."

Damián is a gifted craftsman, despite his crippled hands and twisted fingers. After careful

Damián and Maria in the leper colony in Sapucay, 2013

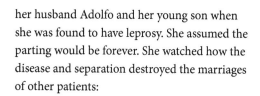

observation of the sun, he carved a sundial out of a stone in his garden that accurately reads the hour, day, and month of the year. But now his eyesight is failing. On a last attempt at carving a wooden figure of Francis of Assisi, he accidentally cut off the saint's fingers. "St. Francis was known as the friend of lepers, so it's appropriate he has no fingers," he jokes. Unable to carve, he now contents himself with carefully tending a garden on the patch of dirt in front of the tiny wooden hut they call home.

Pencil drawings by Maria Weiss

Maria is confined to a wheelchair with one leg amputated and is nearly deaf, but she shows no signs of self-pity. "She is the administrator of the house, and manages everything," says Damián proudly.

The love between them is visible and tender. Damián says they have made it this far only through dialogue, never letting a day end without resolving their differences. Their failing hearing creates new challenges, but they often understand the needs and thoughts of the other instinctively without even talking. "Every day we love each other more, and understand each other better."

The faithfulness of Damián and Maria despite all odds gives witness to a love that lasts; not a passing selfish infatuation but the love described in the well-known verse: "Love is patient, love is kind. It does not envy, it does not boast, it is not proud. It is not rude, it is not self-seeking, it is not easily angered, it keeps no record of wrongs. Love does not delight in evil but rejoices with the truth. It always protects, always trusts, always hopes, always perseveres" (1 Cor. 13:4–7).

Damián and Maria on their wedding day

Another Sapucay patient, Maria Weiss, was separated from

her husband Adolfo and her young son when she was found to have leprosy. She assumed the parting would be forever. She watched how the disease and separation destroyed the marriages of other patients:

> There were always men looking for a partner with whom to set up house. All the women were sought after, no matter what their age. While I was there, two seventy-year-old women married. . . .
>
> One woman was so scared when her husband took leprosy that she moved away and left no address, for she didn't want letters that might carry the infection. But I found couples where the opposite had happened and the wife had accompanied her husband to the colony when he had taken leprosy. There were women in the colony who had lived fifteen or twenty years with severely ill husbands, without taking any precautions to protect themselves, and they had not taken the disease. When I first heard this, I was very surprised and asked how this could be, and I was told, "You won't get it if you are not afraid for your own skin!"
>
> I also noticed that many very poor women living near the colony were only too glad to come and live as wives or *compañeras* to patients, for then they got an assured ration of food free. They were more afraid of hunger than of leprosy.

It would be almost twenty years before Maria was reunited with Adolfo, who had meanwhile joined my community. The trials of life in the leper colony had changed her outlook in surprising ways:

> I found my thoughts had completely changed since those early days in the colony. Then my thoughts were entirely about me or mine. I was sorry for myself and I worried endlessly about my husband and my son. Now I hardly ever thought about myself. I knew that just as God had cared for me all these years, so he could care for my husband and child. So I did not worry anymore but trusted them to His hands,

for I knew He could care for them better than I could.

And I began to realize how many things I would not have known if I had stayed happily at home, with husband, son, house, and farm nearby. For at the colony I was forced to find strength and comfort in the Bible and the hymnal. I had also learned that God can come and give a joy such as I had never heard of when I had all the things around me that folk prize most in life.

In collecting stories for my most recent book, *Rich in Years,* I interviewed dozens of couples who, like Damián and Maria and Adolfo and Maria, had celebrated fifty years together. A few common threads began to emerge. Their lives were not easy; many of them had endured suffering and hardship. Some survived the Great Depression, while others were veterans of the many wars of the last century. Yet, as these stories of love in a leper colony show, hardship can strengthen faith and engender faithfulness. Is it possible that the comfort and affluence we enjoy today might be more of a threat to lifelong marriage than the hardships our parents or grandparents knew?

Perhaps more importantly, most of these couples also had a deep faith in God. They were taught moral values by their parents and teachers in childhood. They stressed the value of listening to one's conscience regarding right and wrong. Their lives show what a difference it can make when a child grows up in a two-parent home – when husband and wife keep their marriage vows for life, "until death parts you." Sadly, my generation has for the most part failed to pass on this legacy to our children.

Does that mean we should be resigned to the fact that the majority of today's marriages will fail to stand the test of time? To be sure, a healthy family life in childhood is the best foundation for any marriage.

But I am convinced that with Christ, and the support of the loving, caring church community that Jesus envisions in his Sermon on the Mount, there is hope for every marriage. ✈

Johann Christoph Arnold is a senior pastor of the Bruderhof communities and author of eleven books, most recently Rich in Years: Finding Peace and Purpose in a Long Life. *www.richinyears.com*

Maria Weiss at her home in Paraguay

INSIGHTS
on the Sermon on the Mount

Blessed Are the Poor in Spirit
MOTHER TERESA

God cannot fill what is full. He can fill only emptiness – deep poverty – and your "yes" [to Jesus] is the beginning of being or becoming empty. It is not how much we really "have" to give – but how empty we are – so that we can receive fully in our life and let him live his life in us. In you today, he wants to relive his complete submission to his father – allow him to do so. Take away your eyes from yourself and rejoice that you have nothing.

Do Not Worry
SØREN KIERKEGAARD

Do not worry about your life. Worrying about making a living, or not making a living, is a snare. In actuality, it is *the* snare. No external power, no actual circumstance, can trap a person. If we choose to be our own providence, then we will go quite ingenuously into our own trap, the wealthy as well as the poor. If we want to entrench ourselves in our own plot of ground that is not under God's care, then we are living, though we do not acknowledge it, in a prison.

Blessed Are the Merciful
HENRI NOUWEN

Blessed are the merciful. Showing mercy is different from having pity. Pity connotes distance, even looking down upon. When a beggar asks for money and you give him something out of pity, you are not showing mercy. Mercy comes from a compassionate heart; it comes from a desire to be an equal. Jesus didn't look down on us. He became one of us and felt deeply with us.

The Light of the World
JOHN WESLEY

You are the light of the world; a city on a hill cannot be hid. Your holiness makes you as conspicuous as the sun in the sky. You cannot hide your Christian character. Love cannot be hidden any more than can light. Least of all, it cannot be hidden when it shines forth in action. When you exercise yourself in a labor of love, in any kind of good work, you are observed. We may as well try to hide a city as to hide a Christian. It is the purpose of God that every Christian should be in open view. He is to give light to all that are in the house.

Sources: Mother Teresa, *Come Be My Light* (Doubleday, 2007), 275. Henri Nouwen, *Bread for the Journey* (Harper One, 1996), May 26. John Wesley, "Upon Our Lord's Sermon on the Mount, Discourse IV," *Forty-four Sermons,* XIX. Søren Kierkegaard, *Provocations,* ed. Charles Moore (Plough, 2002), 148. Artwork: August Macke, *Stilleben: Hyazinthenteppich.*

The Hard Work of the Gospel

LETTERS ON THE SERMON ON THE MOUNT

DOROTHY DAY

"**L**ove your enemies,** do good to those who hate you, and pray for those who persecute you" [Matt. 5:44]. We are at war [World War II]. But still we can repeat Christ's words each day, holding them close in our hearts, and each month printing them in the paper. . . . We are still pacifists.

Our manifesto is the Sermon on the Mount, which means that we will try to be peacemakers. . . . We will try daily, hourly, to pray for an end to the war. Let us add that unless we combine this prayer with almsgiving, in giving to the least of God's children, and fasting in order that we may help feed the hungry, and penance in recognition of our share in the guilt, our prayer may become empty words.

"Unless the seed falls to the ground and die, it remains alone; but if it dies, it brings forth much fruit" [John 12:24]. I don't expect any success. . . . I expect that everything we do [will] be attended with human conflicts, and the suffering that goes with it. . . . I expect that all our natural love for each other which is so warm and encouraging and so much a reward for this kind of work and living, will be killed, put to death painfully by gossip, intrigue, suspicion, distrust, etc. This painful dying to self and to the longing for the love of others will be rewarded by a tremendous increase of supernatural love among us all. I expect the most dangerous of sins to crop up among us, whether of sensuality or pride it does not matter, but that the struggle will go on to such an extent that God will not let it hinder the work. The work will go on, because that work is our suffering and our sanctification. So rejoice in failures, rejoice in suffering!

What are we trying to do? We are trying to get to heaven, all of us. We are trying to lead a good life. We are trying to talk about and write about the Sermon on the Mount, the Beatitudes, the social principles of the church, and it is most astounding, the things that happen when you start trying to live this way.

If we could only learn that the important thing is love, and that we will be judged on love – to keep on loving, and showing that love, and expressing that love, over and over, whether we feel it or not, seventy times seven, to mothers-in-law, to husbands, to children – and to be oblivious of insult, or hurt, or injury – not to see them, not to hear them. It is a hard, hard doctrine. . . . We have got to pray, to read the Gospel, to get to frequent communion, and not judge, not do anything, but love, love, love. A bitter lesson. ➤

From All the Way to Heaven: The Selected Letters of Dorothy Day, *ed. Robert Ellsberg (Image, 2012; hardcover Marquette University Press, 2010).*

DUANE STOLTZFUS

The Martyrs of Alcatraz

Newly discovered letters from World War I pacifists imprisoned for refusing military service shed fresh light on a long-suppressed chapter of American history – and on the meaning of religious liberty today.

When in 1926 President Calvin Coolidge dedicated the Liberty Memorial Tower in Kansas City, Missouri, 150,000 people turned up, setting what was then a record for the largest peacetime crowd ever to gather in the United States. They came to pay homage to the millions of American men inducted into the armed services during a war that began one hundred years ago this August. The inscription on the tower reads: "In honor of those who served in the world war in defense of liberty and our country."[1]

Not included among those honored were four inductees from South Dakota: the three brothers David, Joseph, and Michael Hofer, and Joseph's brother-in-law Jacob Wipf. For refusing to put on a military uniform, the four men, all farmers, ended up hanging in chains at Alcatraz, a treatment that President Woodrow Wilson would later describe in general terms as "barbarous or medieval." Two of them, Joseph and Michael Hofer, died in late 1918 shortly after their transfer to a prison at Fort Leavenworth, Kansas – eight years before the dedication of the Kansas City monument to American liberty.

At the time, their deaths were met with silence. The hometown weekly paper, *The Freeman Courier*, printed a one-sentence death notice on page eight as part of a series of dispatches from the Wolf Creek region: "The two sons of Jacob Hofer of Rockport died in a Wash. camp [sic] and were buried at home."[2] The subject quickly changed. The next item in the column read: "The Neu Hutterthal church decided to buy a paper cutter for Bartel of China"; and below that, "Sam K. Hofer is building a kitchen and auto shed."

Visitors to the cemetery of Rockport Colony, the Hutterite community of which the men were members, will find the grave markers for

Duane C. S. Stoltzfus, professor of communication at Goshen College, is the author of Pacifists in Chains: The Persecution of Hutterites during the Great War *(John Hopkins University Press, 2013). Watercolor illustrations by Don Peters.*

Joseph and Michael of the same dimensions and materials as those on other graves, but with one word appended: *Martyr*.

Jacob Wipf and David, Joseph, and Michael Hofer were called to war on an overcast day on May 25, 1918. At thirty, Jacob was the oldest member of the group, leaving a wife and three children at home. Next oldest was David, twenty-eight, also married with five children, followed by Michael, twenty-four, whose wife Maria had just given birth to a daughter, Mary. The youngest, Joseph, was twenty-three, with a one-year-old and two-year-old at home as well as a baby on the way. When asked by the draft board whether they were the sole providers for the families, each of the men had answered no, since they knew that their church would step in to help if they were gone. With this response, the chance of a near-certain exemption passed them by: fathers of dependent children were almost never drafted.

The four men from the Rockport Colony traveled from their communal home by dirt roads to nearby Alexandria, where scores of their neighbors gathered for a patriotic rally to cheer on all of the young men who were heading off to war. A judge from Sioux Falls delivered the keynote speech that Saturday afternoon, saying that each young man about to board the train for Camp Lewis in Washington was participating in "the fight for freedom and for humanity" and in doing so "proving a loyalty to their country of which every citizen should be proud."[3]

A storm rolled in, and the crowd dashed for cover. When they reconvened, a band led the dignitaries, the soldiers, and their families on a spirited procession to the train station. By all accounts, the young men on the ground in Alexandria were eager to climb aboard the military train, joining hundreds of men who were

already on board and who were leaning out of the windows and waving to the crowd. It was a festive occasion, the start of an adventure for South Dakotans, many of whom were about to see the West for the first time.

A close observer would have noted that the four Hutterites from Rockport Colony and their friend from a neighboring colony, Andrew Wurtz, looked different from the other young men. They were dressed in black and wore beards, visible symbols of their commitment to being separate from the world and focused on living out the peaceable kingdom of God in community. The Hutterites had been directed by their ministers and family members to report to the camp, as required, but to do nothing that would advance the war effort. In no manner were they to serve as soldiers. To do so would be to disobey Christ's commands to love the enemy and reject violence.

Such convictions were sure to earn more hostility than admiration amid the wave of wartime patriotism now sweeping South Dakota and the rest of the nation. Weeks before, the Liberty Loan Committee of nearby Hanson County had illegally confiscated a hundred steers and a thousand sheep from a Hutterite settlement whose members refused to buy war bonds. And on May 25, 1918, the very day that the men left home for Camp Lewis in Washington State, the South Dakota Council of Defense banned the use of German, "the enemy language," in the state.[4] The Hutterites, who both worshipped and taught school in German, were a clear target of the legislation.

Knowing this, the Hofer brothers and Jacob Wipf had reason to be wary as they climbed onto the train to Camp Lewis, joining the 1,200 other young South Dakotans on board. In their own minds, their arrival at the camp would be the moment when they would testify to their faith and their refusal to serve as soldiers. To the American government, however, they had ceased to be civilians from the moment they received their conscription papers.

As the fifteen-car train started heading west, the four men were moved from one Pullman coach to the next. The recruits in each car heckled the Hutterites, who were well known in this part of the country as pacifists and German speakers. The conductor finally found a small compartment where the men could be by themselves.

Joseph Hofer's first letter home, to his wife, Maria, conveys his sense of relief that they found a quiet place on Saturday evening:

Don Peters

> First, a heartfelt greeting and kiss of love. Now, my dear spouse, because it is impossible to speak together in person, I must turn to the pencil and report a bit about how things are going with us. Thank God that we have nothing more to do with the worldly rabble.
>
> Yesterday evening they chased us from our car into another. But we could not stay there so they gave us a small room. So the four of us were there alone. We wanted to also have Andrew Wurtz with us and wanted in our loneliness to be instructed in the fear of God, to be comforted and edified in good things, undisturbed by all the others. For this we cannot thank God enough. Now, dear spouse, we rest contented and commit ourselves into God's hands. He will work out everything for the best.

Later that day, as the train arrived at Judith Basin, Montana, came a knock at the door. A band of fellow recruits wished to speak with the Hutterites, who knew two of the men, William Danforth and James Albert Montgomery, from their

hometown. The Hutterites at first declined to open the door; when they finally agreed to do so, Danforth, Montgomery, and the others stormed into the room. One by one, they forcibly removed the Hutterites, shaving their beards and cutting their hair. The men who stormed the room spoke of administering a "free barbering" intended only to welcome the Hutterites into the ranks of regular soldiers; the Hutterites, on the other hand, felt as if they had been grievously assaulted.[5]

Immediately afterward Michael Hofer wrote to his wife, Maria:

> When we arrived in Judith Basin in Montana they came to us and ordered that we should come out. . . . But we said to them: no, we are not going out unless the captain himself commands it. Then he himself came to us – that is, Danforth, and Montgomery – and ordered Jacob Wipf, saying we should come out and walk over to them. So Jacob Wipf went out. They were already waiting for him and took him into the next car in front of ours and cut

Don Peters

his hair entirely off including his beard. . . . Then they came again . . . and again.

Our Savior has gone before us as an example that we should follow after him in his footsteps, for we have come into such a great suffering. God the almighty alone knows what still awaits us.

The train continued on without further incident, reaching Washington a couple of days later. Recruits from across the West were pouring into Camp Lewis, at seventy thousand acres an impressive army training camp. During the summer of 1917, a work crew of ten thousand men had built in effect a city: 1,757 buildings, fifty miles of roads, and thirty-seven miles of water pipe. On Tuesday, May 28, the Hofer brothers and Jacob Wipf entered this khaki city where tens of thousands of young men were being trained, many of them as infantrymen bound for Europe.

The Hutterites from South Dakota ended up in Guardhouse No. 54 almost immediately. When they arrived, they were told to line up alphabetically in preparation for filling out the enlistment and assignment cards, containing names, hometowns, and other basic information. But the men stepped away from the line, sensing that to do otherwise would be to line up as soldiers in the U.S. Army. They refused to fill out the enlistment and assignment cards, which were titled "Statement of Soldier." Officers tried to persuade the men to follow orders, but to no avail. President Woodrow Wilson and Newton Baker, the secretary of war, expected each man to do his part, even conscientious objectors who might be assigned to kitchen duty or maintenance. The camp commanders seem to have been understandably exasperated by this blanket refusal to participate in camp life.

So while Camp Lewis prepared for war, the Hutterites remained in the guardhouse, awaiting trial.

From the guardhouse, David Hofer wrote to his wife, Anna:

If you think about where we are, far from home and farm, from wife and children, then I can't describe the misery in which we find ourselves. We have already been seriously challenged by various things, but with God's help and remaining faithful to him and our vow not to abandon our promise, let it cost body and life. . . . For our dear Savior says, in Matthew 5, "Blessed are those who are persecuted for righteousness' sake, for the kingdom of God is theirs." I must close now with my simple writing and one has to be careful what we write, and we can't write very often, not as often as we would hope. We are being court-martialed, for five to twenty-five years in jail. . . . So our people should hurry down and perhaps they can do something about it.

The camp authorities charged the Hutterites with disobeying orders, thus violating two of the Articles of War. In the court-martial trial, officers recounted their efforts to persuade the men to line up and fill out the requisite forms. Jacob Wipf was the first defendant to take the stand. An untraveled farmer whose mother tongue was German and who had only a grade-school education, he now had to face a panel of officers. The prosecutor wanted to know exactly why the men would not serve in the armed forces in any capacity.

Q: Are you willing to take part in any noncombatant branch of the service of the army?

A: No; we can't.

Q: What are your reasons?

A: Well, it is all for war. The only thing we can do is work on a farm for the poor and needy ones of the United States.

Q: What do you mean by poor and needy ones?

A: Well, those that can't help themselves.

Q: Would you include soldiers who are crippled for life?

Discovering the Hofer Brothers' Letters

Duane Stoltzfus

When researching the story of the Hofer brothers and Jacob Wipf for my book Pacifists in Chains *(John Hopkins University Press, 2013), I experienced a moment of drama: the discovery that the letters by the Hofer brothers still survived. Family members in Montana and Saskatchewan allowed me to see copies of seventy-nine letters that had been in their possession since the war.* Of that number, the brothers wrote fifty-nine and received twenty. These copies appear here as illustrations. (No comparable packet of prison letters written by Jacob Wipf has turned up.)*

The brothers began writing on May 26, 1918, when they were en route to Camp Lewis. The saved correspondence is heaviest in the month of June, when they were court-martialed and locked up in the guardhouse at Camp Lewis, awaiting transfer to Alcatraz. The letters shed light on their experiences through subsequent months of captivity. Michael and Joseph Hofer wrote their last letters in the collection to their wives, both named Maria, on November 17, 1918, while they were traveling from Alcatraz to Fort Leavenworth. Little more than two weeks later, both men were dead.

Michael Hofer's last letter to his wife Maria. Family members copied out the Hofer brothers' correspondence; the original letters seem to have been buried with the men or their spouses.

---

* Family members living at the Miller Colony in Choteau, Montana; the Kingsbury Colony in Valier, Montana; and the Kyle Colony in Kyle, Saskatchewan, provided copies of the letters.

A: Yes. They are poor and needy ones. . . .

Q: If you were in the service, such as the Medical Corps, where you would attend the wounded soldiers, would your conscience and the teachings of the church permit that?

A: We can't do that, because a soldier, he will go and fight, and that is helping the war, and we can't do that.

Q: And if there were wounded soldiers about, you couldn't help them? You couldn't help them because you would be afraid they might recover and go back to the war; is that it?

A: Well, it would be helping the war.

Q: Would you be willing to be placed on a farm by the government and grow wheat for soldiers?

A: No.

The prosecutor then wanted to know if the commitment to nonviolence extended to the home.

Q: Does your religion believe in fighting of any kind?

A: No.

Q: You would not fight with your fists?

A: Well, we ain't no angels. Little boys will scrap sometimes, and we are punished; but our religion don't allow it.

Q: To put the case like this: If a man was attacking or assaulting your sister, would you fight?

A: No.

Q: Would you kill him?

A: No.

Q: What would you do?

A: Well, in a way, if I could get her away, I might hold him. If I was man enough, I would do that. If I couldn't, I would have to let go. We can't kill. That is strictly against our religion.

The Hofer brothers, in turn, testified as well, and then the four waited for the decision. David Hofer wrote to tell Anna about the trial:

> That was a difficult test. Dear spouse, that is something our dear brothers, fathers, and patriarchs never had to do, what we young brothers in faith had to do. We had to defend our beliefs in front of the twelve jurors. But

Liberty Memorial at the National World War I Museum, Kansas City, Missouri

Remembering Muted Voices
Conscience, Dissent, Resistance and Civil Liberties in World War I through Today

October 19-21, 2017, National World War I Museum, Kansas City, Missouri

Nearly one hundred years after the end of World War I, the story of these four conscientious objectors is poised to be told in what may seem to be among the most unlikely of places: the National World War I Museum at Liberty Memorial in Kansas City, Missouri. In 2004, Congress designated it as the nation's official World War I museum; more than one million people have visited since it opened in 2006. The museum is home to one of the largest Great War collections in the world, exceeding seventy-five thousand items.

The museum plans to host a conference in 2017 that will explore the experiences of groups and individuals who voiced their objections to the war, sometimes at great cost. Titled "Remembering Muted Voices: Conscience, Dissent, Resistance and Civil Liberties in World War I through Today," the conference will include the story of the Hofer brothers and Jacob Wipf, in conjunction with a traveling exhibition. *www.theworldwar.org*

God stood at our side, and gave us voice and wisdom and a calm heart. I had no more fear than I would have if I were at home. . . . Dear spouse, if only our heavenly Father could lead us out of this misery, no matter where, even if into dire poverty.

The verdict arrived five days after the trial, less than three weeks after the men had arrived at Camp Lewis. All four men were found guilty of all charges; the sentence was dishonorable discharge, loss of all pay, and prison. Michael Hofer shared the news with Maria:

On Saturday they came and announced to us our punishment, namely, twenty years of hard labor in the prison at Alcatraz, California. God the heavenly Father knows what still awaits us. But we must put our trust in him and accept with patience whatever he allows to happen to us. We are completely yielded to the Lord. Whatever burdens he gives, he also provides a way out so that we can endure it. . . . We only make our cross and suffering more difficult if we are sad. For God will also be with us there (that is, in Alcatraz). He has promised to his own, that when they pass through the fire, he will stand beside them so that the flames do not burn them.

The Hofer brothers and Jacob Wipf were among 504 conscientious objectors who were court-martialed during the war, resulting in 503 convictions and a single acquittal. Of the men who were court-martialed, about 142 were believed to be Mennonite, Amish, or Hutterite. Meanwhile, Andrew Wurtz, who had been separated from the Hofer brothers and Jacob Wipf after their arrival at Camp Lewis, faced his own trial. He described extreme physical measures applied to persuade him to work: being forcibly dunked in cold water, being pulled across floor boards to drive splinters into his skin, and more. Eventually he agreed to work in the camp garden, but only alone, not in the company of men in uniform.

After two months at Camp Lewis, on July 25, the Hofer brothers and Jacob Wipf left for Alcatraz. They were chained together in pairs and traveled in the escort of four armed lieutenants, arriving two days later at the notorious island in San Francisco Bay. Known as "the Rock," and formally designated as the "United States Disciplinary Barracks, Pacific Branch," Alcatraz was one of three detention centers for military prisoners. It was known for its liberal management. Under its commandant, Colonel Garrard, inmates – referred to as "disciples" – enjoyed access to vocational training programs, classical concerts, and a library boasting 4600 books (as well as, incongruously, a complete set of the *Ladies Home Journal* for 1917). As the four Hutterites would soon find out, however, this liberalism did not extend to conscientious objectors, who were scorned as "slackers."

On arrival, the four men climbed a series of switchbacks to reach the cell house on top of the island. Once inside they were unwilling to put on uniforms or to work.

Guards took them along a corridor of stacked cells to a staircase that led to the basement of the prison, the dungeon, a place of solitary confinement known as "the hole." Each man entered a cell under a sloping brick arch, six feet high at the uppermost point; the cell itself measured six and a half feet wide by eight feet deep. The cells were cold and wet, but the men declined to put on the uniforms that lay on the floor beside them. In the early days, the men received half a glass of water each day but no food.

Days after their arrival the men found themselves chained to the bars in their respective doors, one hand crossed over the other. The chains were drawn up so that only their toes touched the floor, a technique long familiar in the history of torture known as "high cuffing."

Don Peters

David Hofer said that he tried to move the toilet pail closer so that he could stand on it to relieve the pain in his arms. Living in darkness by day and by night, the men received periodic visits from guards. At least once the guards reportedly came with knotted lashes and hit the men on the arms and back. When the guards led the men to an outside yard after the first five days in solitary confinement, the four men tried without success to put on their jackets; their arms were too swollen.

From Alcatraz, Joseph Hofer shared only a sense of general hardship in writing to his wife, Maria. Like his brothers, Joseph omitted details of their solitary imprisonment; or it may be that prison officials excised any unpleasant or incriminating details from the outgoing letters.

> I am still in good health, both physically and spiritually. . . . My precious and dear wife, I am

still in prison and I do not know if we will ever see each other again. Let us hope that we will; but if not in this world, then in that yonder place where no one will separate us from each other.

But in order to get there we must put off all desires of the flesh, and take the cross upon ourselves, along with the hatred and taunting of the world, and look up to Jesus our Savior and to his apostles, and to our forefathers, as Paul says in Hebrews 12. For we have a cloud of witnesses before us. And you will find there that all those who found pleasure with God had to suffer affliction.

Now, my best wishes to you and to all those who read this letter. Amen. Here everything is militaristic, as it was in the camp.

The Hofer brothers (or, as they were known here, Nos. 15238, 15239, and 15240) and Jacob Wipf (No. 15237) provided scarcely a glimpse at this time of their traumatic life at Alcatraz. There is no mention in the letters of sleeping on wet concrete in their underwear, of standing for hours in chains, or of being beaten by guards. Instead, Michael Hofer wrote home:

> My dear spouse, if we no longer see each other in this world, then it is my hope in God that it will happen in the next world where no one will be able to separate us – where we will remain forever in joy.

On Armistice Day, November 11, 1918, residents gathered in San Francisco to celebrate the end of the war with rounds of "Auld Lang Syne." They sang with flu masks on, a visible reminder of the influenza epidemic that had swept across the country. But this was a time to revel in the news. Three days after the armistice, the Hutterites left for Fort Leavenworth, once more in chains and escorted by armed officers. During the train ride, Michael Hofer wrote his final letter:

Entrance to Camp Lewis, Washington, where the Hofer brothers and Jacob Wipf refused to don the military uniform. *Kirtland Cutter, January 1918; Courtesy Fort Lewis Museum.*

Alcatraz Island, "the Rock," 1902–1905. Contrary to its later reputation, Alcatraz in 1918 was known as a progressive institution–at least for prisoners who complied with regulations. *Jack W. Fleming, Golden Gate NRA, Park Archives.*

Far left: "The hole," in Alcatraz, where the four conscientious objectors were kept in solitary confinement for two-week stretches on a bread-and-water diet, shackled to the bars of their cells. (Some years later, the bars were removed.) *www.the-rock.sl/documentation/dungeons-of-alcatraz/*

Left: Stairway leading underground to "the hole." *Courtesy Duane Stoltzfus, 2013.*

Grave markers in Rockport colony, South Dakota. *Courtesy Bruderhof Historical Archive.*

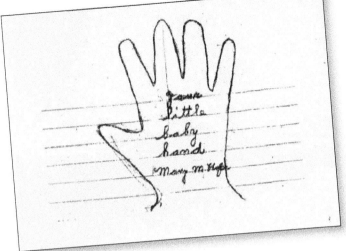

Michael Hofer's wife sent him this hand sketch of their daughter. "Baby Mary" was one and a half years old when her father died.

Grace and peace be with you. I want to write to you that we are now on the way to Fort Leavenworth. We don't know, however, what will become of us there. Only God the Almighty knows if we will see each other again in this world, for we go from one affliction to the other. We plead earnestly to God, for he has promised us that not a single hair falls from our heads without his will. And if we do not see each other again in this world, then we will see one another in the next world.

Joseph, likewise, wrote his final letter home, to Maria:

And when you look at our scrawling you can well imagine how low our spirits are, for we are where the waves are roaring and in that time when the seas throw up the dead – if you can only see this in the right way.

This is all for this time, my dear wife. For this is not a good letter at all, since the train shakes and bounces so much. Now to close. My best greetings to you and our dear children, father and mother and all the brothers and sisters in the faith.

The men arrived at Fort Leavenworth on November 19 around midnight. Though the accounts of what happened next differ, David Hofer described a march through the streets to the barracks and then a long wait outdoors before prison clothing arrived. Michael and Joseph Hofer complained of sharp pains in the chest soon after their arrival; they were

transferred to the hospital. David Hofer and Jacob Wipf, meanwhile, were held, once again, in solitary confinement when they said they could do no work at Fort Leavenworth.

When Michael's and Joseph's condition deteriorated, David sent a telegram urging family members to come quickly. They arrived on November 28, finding Joseph barely able to communicate and Michael in not much better condition. The following morning, when Joseph's wife, Maria, went to see him, she discovered that he was dead. At first prison officials did not want to let her through to see his body. She persisted and found, to her dismay, in approaching the coffin, that in death he had been dressed in a military uniform. A few days later, on December 2, Michael Hofer died. David was released to accompany the bodies of his brothers back to South Dakota.

The Office of the Surgeon of the Disciplinary Barracks listed pneumonia as the cause of death for both men, a common designation for the "Spanish" influenza then sweeping through the prison, as it had across San Francisco when the men were held at Alcatraz. In contrast, the Hutterite church was convinced that the men died because of mistreatment in the months leading up to their deaths. *The Chronicle of the Hutterian Brethren* states that the men "died in prison as a result of cruel mistreatment by the United States military."[6]

No representative of the United States government ever apologized to the Hofer brothers' families, who would later emigrate to Canada. Fellow church members were quick to absolve President Wilson and Secretary of War Newton Baker of direct responsibility, blaming overzealous generals at the recruitment camps. Other observers were less forgiving. Frank Harris, the cosmopolitan editor of the *Saturday Review,* would write in his memoir:

Is there any doubt as to who is the better man, the brothers Hofer who went through martyrdom to death for their noble belief, or Secretary Baker, who was responsible for their murder? After the facts had been brought before the Secretary [of War] again and again, month after month, day after day, at long last, on December 6, 1918, nearly a month after the war was ended, Secretary Baker found time to issue an order prohibiting cruel corporal punishment, and the handcuffing of prisoners to the bars of their dungeons, etc. Secretary Baker already knew such torture was being practiced, knew too that it was illegal.[7]

For his part, Baker would likely have retorted that Harris was willfully ignorant of what it takes to speedily mobilize an army in a war where every day counts. He himself expressed few regrets: "I knew the horror of [war] . . . and I have no sympathy whatever, intellectually or sentimentally, with conscientious or any other kind of objection of people who stayed on this side and preferred place of safety and profit to places of peril and obligation."[8]

When Jacob Wipf was finally released from his "place of safety and profit" in April of 1919, he saw his comrades' graves for himself. Granted clemency by the Office of the Judge Advocate General of the Army, he came home eleven months after his arrest, just in time for spring planting. ⤳

1. Quotes and other information on the National World War I Museum at Liberty Memorial are drawn from the museum's website at *www.theworldwar.org*.

2. "Wolf Creek," *The Freeman Courier,* December 5, 1918.

3. *The Alexandria Herald,* May 31, 1918.

4. *The Alexandria Herald,* May 31, 1918.

5. *The Alexandria Herald,* June 21, 1918.

6. *The Chronicle of the Hutterian Brethren,* vol. 1. (Rifton, NY: Plough Publishing, 1987), 807.

7. Frank Harris, *My Life and Loves* (New York: Grove Press, 1963), 946.

8. Reply from Newton D. Baker to socialist convention, Baker Papers, 1918–1919 (no date specified).

Becoming a People
Cultivating Christian Community

C. CHRISTOPHER SMITH

What will happen to our churches if we get serious about the Sermon on the Mount – not just as a discussion starter, but as a roadmap for our life together? Almost two decades ago, Englewood Christian Community Church in Indianapolis decided to take the first steps on this exciting journey. We asked author and Englewood member C. Christopher Smith what he's learned.

The Sermon on the Mount is the key to understanding who Jesus was and what it means to follow in his way. Yet we struggle to know how it pertains to our lives today. Formed by the prevailing individualism of Western culture, we try to read the Sermon as a set of personal instructions – and we fail. Often we accept that the way of life described here is the way that Jesus intends for us, but amidst our fragmented daily routine we lose hope of actually being able to live accordingly. When it comes to the harder teachings of Jesus – "Love your enemies," "Do not worry about tomorrow" – we may even rationalize why we don't have to have to take his words seriously.

Yet Jesus' teachings in the Sermon on the Mount were not meant primarily for us as individuals. Rather, they offer a vision of what maturity in Christ looks like for our church communities. As German theologian Gerhard Lohfink reminds us, God's redemptive work in the world consists in the gathering of a people.[1] This work began with ancient Israel, the descendants of Abraham, Isaac, and Jacob, and was carried forward by Jesus, who gathered a little community of twelve disciples as a symbol of the twelve tribes of Israel. After Pentecost, when these disciples were sent out, Gentiles were invited to be part of God's people as well as Jews, and the people of God was no longer defined by ethnicity.

In light of this community-building mission of God, what the Sermon on the Mount offers us is not a new law by which to judge ourselves or others, but rather a vision of what it means to embody Christ. The teachings in the Sermon show us, above all, how we are to live with our

1. See for example Gerhard Lohfink, *Jesus and Community* (Fortress, 1984).

sisters and brothers in our church community, sharing life together in a way that is different from that of mainstream culture. We must pay attention to the many times Jesus says, "You have heard it said . . . but I say to you. . . ." With this rhetorical pattern, Jesus paints a contrast between the way of God's people and the way of the world. He makes the same point by means of the imagery of salt and light: these are likewise images of contrast.

The ethics of the Sermon on the Mount are rooted in the slow, transforming work of God that begins with particular communities of God's people and spreads outward from there. Perhaps this is one meaning of Jesus' words, "Do not judge," and "First take the log out of your own eye, and then you will see clearly to take the speck out of your brother's eye" (Matt. 7:1–5). Our church communities need to focus on getting the log out of our own eye by seeking to embody Jesus together and living in the way that he taught us, rather than judging or trying to fix our neighbors (or the world). We are called to love our neighbors and even our enemies – but we demonstrate that love best by allowing them to see how the transforming wisdom of Jesus is at work in the midst of our church community.

How then do we embody Jesus together in our churches in ways that draw us deeper into the wisdom of the Sermon on the Mount? For over a decade, I've been a member of Englewood Christian Community Church, an urban congregation in Indianapolis. Our shared search on these questions suggests three practices that can give us a good start in the right direction: *stability, conversation, and rhythms of work and Sabbath.* These are each "patient" practices because they

compel us not only to seek the things that Jesus sought, but also to do so in the way he sought them – including his choice to suffer rather than inflict violence. As Eugene Peterson has written:

> If we want to participate (and not just go off in a corner and do our own Jesus thing), participate in the end, the salvation, the kingdom of God, we must do it in the way that is appropriate to that end. We follow Jesus.[2]

These three practices teach us to follow in the patient way of Jesus.

If the primary work that God is doing in the world is indeed one of gathering a people, then it is essential that we value rootedness in a church community and a place: a practice that the Benedictines have called stability. For instance, the Benedictine monks of Our Lady of the Mississippi Abbey in Dubuque, Iowa describe their commitment to stability in this way:

> We vow to remain all our life with our local community. We live together, pray together, work together, relax together. We give up the temptation to move from place to place in search of an ideal situation. Ultimately there is no escape from oneself, and the idea that things would be better someplace else is usually an illusion. And when interpersonal conflicts arise, we have a great incentive to work things out and restore peace. This means learning the practices of love: acknowledging one's own offensive behavior, giving up one's preferences, forgiving.

I have certainly suffered the effects of a lack of stability. In the decade prior to coming to the Englewood church community, I lived at twelve different addresses in four states. Raised in a thoroughly individualist ethos, I spent my

---

2. Eugene H. Peterson, *The Jesus Way: A Conversation on the Ways Jesus Is the Way* (Eerdmans, 2007), 7.

twenties following the narrative of self, choosing the educational and career opportunities that seemed best for me: college, summer internships, a full-time job in a global corporation, grad school, and an internship with a church. Though I made many friends along the way, I paid a price for chasing that story. I was isolated, disconnected from any particular place and community of people. If we are indeed called to embody Christ together, as the Apostle Paul maintains (1 Cor. 12:12–31), then how healthy a body will we be if our members frequently move from one church community to another? As the Benedictine vow reminds us, it is through stability that we learn to practice peacemaking and to be reconciled with one another at all costs.

In addition to the stability of our members, we also need to commit to stability as congregations. Great damage can be done by churches relocating, creating a void that contributes to economic and racial injustice in the neighborhoods they leave behind. We have much to learn from the parish system of Catholicism, in which church and neighborhood are interwoven. Saint Philip Neri parish in my neighborhood, for instance, recently celebrated its hundredth anniversary, having persisted in the same location despite challenges including severe persecution from the Ku Klux Klan in its early years and a drastic shift in its demographics over the last quarter century from a mostly white to a mostly Hispanic congregation.

A second practice that can help us mature into a deeper embodiment of Christ is conversation. Although not typically thought of as an essential Christian practice, conversation is ever more necessary in an atomized culture that is rapidly losing the capacity for real dialogue – the escalating partisanship of the United States Congress in recent years is an obvious example. Conversation is the way in which we actively seek to be faithful together, an expression of our shared hunger and thirst for righteousness. If I may expand on Paul's image of the body, just as there is an ongoing "conversation" of neurons that guides the movement of every bodily organ, so too there should be an ever-present exchange between the members of our church body that is directed by Christ, our head.

Conversation is essential to our understanding and interpreting the scriptural story in our churches. Through reading the Bible in dialogue with each other, we sort through the theological heritage we have as a congregation (and as individuals) while discerning our vocation as God's people in a particular place. Tim Conder and Daniel Rhodes of the Emmaus Way community in Durham, North Carolina, note how gathering to interpret scripture together has changed their life together:

> [We] have developed a passion for the intersection of word and community as well as our distinct willingness to hear each other's voices. This is not an innate skill. It's a learned practice that we've worked hard to cultivate. . . . We believe that many of the strengths of our community are due to this commitment to a community hermeneutic. [3]

Almost twenty years ago, the Englewood church stopped our traditional Sunday night church service. Instead, our members circled up chairs in one of our multi-purpose rooms and began a conversation that continues on Sunday nights to this day. At first these meetings were volatile – yelling, sarcasm, people walking out, a few even

---

3. Tim Conder and Daniel Rhodes, *Free for All: Rediscovering the Bible in Community* (Baker, 2009), 85.

leaving the church altogether – but we have persisted in this practice and have been transformed by it. Conversation did not magically solve all our problems, but it taught us how to trust one another and to work together even when we had substantial disagreements about theology or practical applications.

As we continued to talk together each Sunday, we found ourselves starting to work together on a variety of common endeavors during the week. These became ways for us to extend the conversation into everyday life and help keep it grounded in concrete realities. Unexpectedly, we found that in this way we were being equipped to help lead a broader conversation with other area residents as we sought to envision a flourishing future for our neighborhood. This part of Indianapolis had been abandoned by many businesses, churches, and families. But thanks to this growing dialogue, our neighborhood is slowly beginning to flourish, and we are delighted that we have been called to bear witness to God's transforming love here in this place.

A third practice that draws us into deeper life in Christ is establishing rhythms of work and Sabbath. While our technological age tempts us to minimize inconvenience and exertion, if we seek to embody Christ together it will require diligent work. On the other hand, we are not to be consumed with the anxiety of work (Matt. 6:25–33); rather, we are to trust in God's continual provision for us. We need Sabbath spaces in our life together in which we cease working and can rest, play, dream, and reflect together. One symptom of our individualistic culture is that most of what is written today about Sabbath is directed toward individuals and families. But originally the Sabbath was

instituted as a *social* practice, one that gave shape to the Israelite people of God. We have much to learn from Judaism about what it means to keep the Sabbath as a community. Traditionally, Shabbat has been celebrated with three festive meals, with singing, socializing with friends and family, with contemplation, and with gathered prayer at the synagogue. Even today, in many Jewish communities it remains a day of celebration, the "queen" among the days.

For us at Englewood, common work is an important part of our shared life; we have a daycare, a community development corporation, bookkeeping and publishing businesses, and other not-for-profit ventures. But like many churches today, we struggle to imagine what keeping the Sabbath as a community might look like. As a result, we are often a pretty tired community. Perhaps the closest we come to a shared practice of Sabbath is the Sunday night conversation I've described. Here we cease working, learn to reflect together, and get to know one another better. For many of us, this conversation is the high point of our week, not unlike the Jewish Shabbat, and we are hopeful that our understanding of Sabbath will continue to deepen.

These three practices, if undertaken diligently in our churches, can be first steps on "the narrow way that leads to life" (Matt. 7:14), the life of blessedness and peace with humanity and all creation that Jesus envisions for us in the Sermon on the Mount. ⬎

C. Christopher Smith is co-author, with John Pattison, of Slow Church: Cultivating Community in the Patient Way of Jesus *(IVP Books, June 2014) and editor of* The Englewood Review of Books. *www.englewoodreview.org*

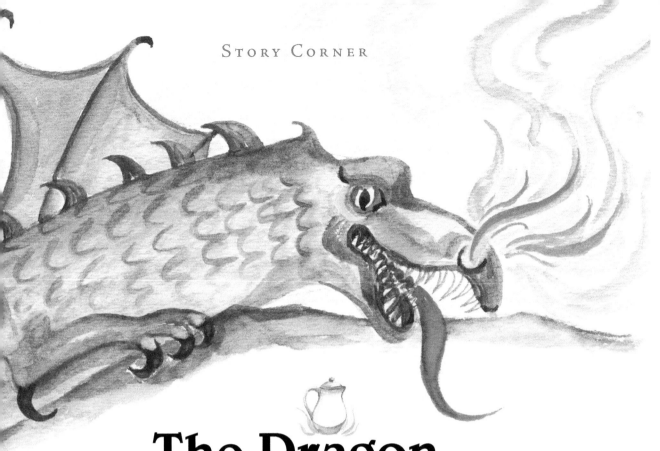

The Dragon
and the Coffee Pot

A Story by Manfred Kyber

Translated by J. Heinrich Arnold • Illustrated by Hannah Marsden

I n a large, deep forest a long time ago, there lived a terrible dragon. He spat poison and he breathed fire from the holes in his nose. He ate people and animals in a way that was sad to see. Dragons are most unfriendly beings who spit poison and eat people and animals. Because of all this, we should not be too surprised that this dragon did the same, for he had no better education than this – and the education of a dragon is not sufficient for a decent life.

It surely was not pleasant to see him sitting there in the forest eating everything that came his way. He only left the bones. Actually, he spat them out and left them lying around the place in a most disorderly fashion. It was a miserable sight and the people of the area were not at all satisfied with the situation.

Upcoming issues of Plough Quarterly *will include more read-aloud stories for young and old.*

One day, a little girl went into this forest to find some berries. Her search led her deeper and deeper into the forest. It was already quite late by the time the girl noticed that she should have been home a long time ago. The darkness was creeping in, and the trees had long, dark shadows. Far away, the girl could hear the church bell of her village. The sound gave her a shock. She was only a very little girl, and she decided to go home fast. She knew that the shortest way would lead her past the home of the dragon. She thought she had to take the shortest way because night was coming fast, and she was afraid of the darkness.

The little girl knew that her parents were waiting at home and that her mother would be worried about her. That is why she decided to go the shortest way. She asked her guardian angel to protect her when she passed near the home of the dragon. She had only just thought of her guardian angel when he already stood next to her.

"Good evening," he said, "the way you go is the path on which the dragon sits."

"I know, I know," said the little girl. "I also know that he is unfriendly and that he eats men and animals, that he spits poison, and that he breathes fire. All this is not nice, but I have to go this way, otherwise I will come home too late. I thought you would protect me in any case."

"This I will do," said the angel, "and I will watch over you, and the dragon will not be able to harm you. But you will see him, if you go this way, and it will be a horrible and shocking sight. Because of this I would prefer it if you would choose a different way."

"I would like to be home before dark, and since you will protect me, it will be all right," said the little girl. "Perhaps the dragon went for a little walk, and perhaps he is not at home. Then I would not even see him."

"So many people who walk on the road of the dragon say the same thing," said the angel, "but the dragon has not gone for a walk. He sits where he always sits, and if you go this way against my advice, then you will see him."

"That is not good," said the little girl. "What shall I do?"

"You must think of your angel, and you should have no fear," said the angel. "Look here, little child, people should never fear dragons. If people would have no fear, then the dragons would become quite small. Then it would not help them a bit that they spit poison and breathe fire."

"I will try to do that. I will think of you, and I will have no fear," said the little girl.

And that is how she walked into the darkness of the forest. The angel disappeared, and the girl felt quite alone. In reality, the angel never left the girl, but she could not see him anymore. It did not take very long before the little girl heard a coughing and a blowing of the nose going on in a most impolite manner.

It was the dragon who spat poison and breathed fire. When the little girl came around the corner, she saw the dragon sitting there on the ground. He was constantly hitting the ground with his ugly tail. On his short clumsy feet were long claws. He was busy just spitting poison and breathing fire, which came out of the holes of his nose. Around the dragon were strewn the bones of many animals. This surely looked disorderly and most distasteful.

The little girl had a shock, but she thought of the angel and tried not to have fear. But it did not seem to work so well.

"It is not nice, the way you behave," said the little girl. "Let me pass by."

"I will not let you pass," said the dragon, and he lay down directly in the path which the girl had to take.

"I will talk with him a little," thought the girl. "Perhaps he will become more reasonable and allow me to pass by. He cannot harm me anyway, because my

angel told me so."

"Tell me, why do you eat people?" asked the little girl. "Do you think that is good manners? Or is it nice if everyone fears you? Can't you eat potato soup? You would only need to put the soup pot on one of the holes in your nose, and the soup would be ready in half an hour. You don't even have to do the work we do to cook our soup."

"Potato soup?" asked the dragon. And he smiled in a very distasteful way, for in smiling he showed his teeth. Just one of his teeth would have been enough to scare a strong man. Potato soup had never been offered to that dragon before.

"Yes, potato soup," said the little girl. "Potato soup is something fine. It is a sign of poor upbringing that you don't like it. You can also drink coffee and have my cookies. I still have coffee in my jug and cookies in my basket. I'll put both here and you can have them. But you have to let me pass by."

"I will eat you," said the dragon.

"Under no circumstances," said the little girl. "You cannot do that because my angel will not give you permission."

"I will not ask your angel," said the dragon.

"Maybe he won't ask the angel after all," thought the little girl, and fear came over her.

"Look how I can flap my wings," said the dragon. "I'll take you into the air."

"You surely cannot fly," said the little girl. "To be able to fly you would have to be a bird or an angel. You do not have real wings. Your wings are short, and they're not even beautiful."

The dragon did not like this at all, because dragons want to be respected. They cannot laugh about themselves. He looked with horrible eyes at the little girl. The little girl's heart was beating like a hammer, but she did not want to be afraid because the angel had told her not to.

"Look how I can use my haunches," said the dragon. "I only need to make one jump, and I'll have you."

"That would be a sign of poor upbringing," said the girl, but she put her hands on her heart and called for her angel.

Suddenly the angel appeared, and around him were many other angels. They did not allow the dragon to come close to the girl. The girl no longer had any fear at all, and suddenly it seemed as if the dragon became smaller and smaller.

"You with your short clumsy legs of a dachshund," said the girl, "you're uneducated! Don't you see the angels around me? How will you be able to come close to me? Drink the coffee and eat the cookies and learn to behave properly."

When the little girl had said this, the angels disappeared, and the forest became quite dark. The dragon, however, had become quite small. He had put the coffee pot on his nose to warm the coffee a little. He almost looked like a little dachshund, and the girl had a good laugh.

"Do you like it?" the girl asked the dragon. For the coffee had begun to boil and steam on the nose of the dragon. The dragon had a good warm meal. The girl took the coffee pot, said good night, and went home.

The bells of the church were still ringing because it had only been a short time that the girl was with the dragon. This is always true when we experience something great.

From that time on, both people and animals were saved from that dragon. He remained as small as a dachshund and he lived on potato soup.

There are many roads in life that lead close to a dangerous dragon. It is of greatest importance at such times to think of our guardian angels. Then the most dangerous dragon becomes quite small, like a little dog, and eats only potato soup.

Manfred Kyber (1880–1933) was a Baltic poet best known for his animal fables. Born in Riga, he moved to Germany to work as a writer and became a pioneering advocate for the ethical treatment of animals.

Was Bonhoeffer Willing to Kill?

CHARLES E. MOORE

The Bonhoeffer family residence in Berlin: the study

Bonhoeffer the Assassin? Challenging the Myth, Recovering His Call to Peacemaking
By Mark Thiessen Nation, Anthony G. Siegrist, Daniel P. Umbel (Baker Academic)

"But what about Bonhoeffer?" It's a challenge thrown out to anyone who, under the impact of Jesus' teaching of nonresistance and love of enemy in the Sermon on the Mount, becomes a pacifist. On the one hand, the four gospels and other early Christian writings seem to teach straightforwardly that Jesus' disciples should be willing to die but never willing to kill.[1] On the other hand, a just-war tradition going back to Augustine or earlier attempts to explain why, as a practical matter, this one aspect of Jesus' teaching should be qualified, bracketed out, or suspended until the Second Coming.

Whatever the virtues of the just-war tradition, it remains notoriously difficult to harmonize with the words and example of Jesus himself as recorded in the New Testament. Perhaps because of this, in recent decades proponents are likely, sooner or later, to invoke the martyr Dietrich Bonhoeffer. A pastor and theologian who died resisting Nazism, Bonhoeffer's name works as an argument-clincher because of his dramatic conversion to "realism": faced with the horror of Germany's crimes during World War II, he abandoned his earlier pacifism and joined a conspiracy to kill Hitler. He thus modeled the kind of responsible decision-making, freed from literalistic scruples, that is the starting point for the just-war tradition.

So runs the standard account of Bonhoeffer's legacy. It's a powerful story, but according to the authors of *Bonhoeffer the Assassin?*, it simply isn't true.

To dislodge a narrative so deeply entrenched in popular perception is a herculean task. Nation, Siegrist, and Umbel go about it thoughtfully, meticulously, and artfully, taking pains to demonstrate how Bonhoeffer was an altogether different kind of martyr than what most people believe. Their claim: Up until his death at the hands of a Nazi executioner in April 1945, Bonhoeffer remained a pacifist, a nonviolent disciple of the crucified Christ who calls his followers to live out the "intolerable offense" of loving one's enemies.

---

1. See Richard Hays's classic *The Moral Vision of the New Testament* (HarperOne, 1996) and Ronald J. Sider's *The Early Church on Killing* (Baker, 2012).

Dietrich Bonhoeffer around the time he took a year's study at Union Theological Seminary in New York (ca. 1931)

In making this argument, the authors certainly have their work cut out for them.

They take the reader step-by-step through Bonhoeffer's life (Part 1) and then his written body of thought (Part 2), methodically unraveling the knots of faulty assumptions that underlie the standard account. For instance, they demolish the assumption that Bonhoeffer's work with the Abwehr, Germany's military intelligence, necessarily shows active involvement in the plot to kill Hitler. They then carefully weave together threads of fact which indicate that Bonhoeffer actually used his position in the Abwehr to oppose Hitler in *nonviolent* ways.

To make their case, the authors examine the biographical evidence in detail. First, Bonhoeffer travelled to the United States in 1939 to avoid military conscription. Upon his return to Germany, he applied to be a military chaplain for precisely the same reason (his application was denied), and then joined the Abwehr knowing that by doing so he would gain an exemption. Bonhoeffer's intelligence post was a cover, allowing him not only to avoid military service but also to continue his work as a pastor, theologian and ecumenical leader of the Confessing Church; trips undertaken for the Abwehr gave Bonhoeffer one of the few avenues still open to him to encourage church leaders in their resistance to the Nazis. According to the authors, his activities contributed nothing positive either to the military efforts of Germany or to the efforts to assassinate Hitler.

The authors conclude that, although Bonhoeffer was aware of various plots to kill Hitler – he knew of five assassination plots, out of the forty-two documented by historians – he himself was never an active participant in any of them: "There is not a shred of evidence that Bonhoeffer was linked in any way to these attempts on Hitler's life" (86). Just because Bonhoeffer engaged in sensitive conversations with the would-be assassins, they argue, it does not follow that he personally participated in their plans.

Since Bonhoeffer's arrest occurred shortly after the discovery of a failed assassination attempt which he knew of, it's often assumed that he was arrested as a conspirator. Official documents, however, tell a different story: Bonhoeffer was arrested because of his involvement in Operation 7, a nonviolent if technically fraudulent scheme to help fourteen Jewish men and women escape Germany. When he was finally indicted in September, he was charged with misusing his position in the Abwehr to evade conscription – thus "subverting military power" – and with making efforts "to keep others from fulfilling military service entirely" (87). To put it anachronistically, the Nazis arrested Bonhoeffer not as a would-be assassin but as a draft dodger.

These charges were not without basis, as the authors show. Reviewing Bonhoeffer's letters, sermons, and various other writings from the mid-1930s onward, they argue that he not only remained committed to nonviolence himself, but also sought to influence his students and others to consider being conscientious objectors. As late as 1942, just months before his arrest, Bonhoeffer wrote to his close friend Eberhard Bethge that he stood behind what he had written in *Discipleship,* the book in which he had unequivocally espoused pacifism.

Having followed the historical trail as far as it would take them, the authors turn next to Bonhoeffer's writings. Was his commitment to nonviolence absolute, or did he come to believe that under certain circumstances violence could be justified? The standard account, influenced by Reinhold Niebuhr's categories of realism and responsibility, interprets Bonhoeffer's participation in the Abwehr as indicative of – or perhaps as a catalyst for – an ethical and theological shift. Bonhoeffer, it is said, changed his mind, rejecting his earlier insistence on nonviolence in favor of a more realistic moral calculus, one that recognizes that there are tragic situations in which choosing the lesser evil is the best a Christian can do.

This shift, according to this interpretation, is apparent when one compares Bonhoeffer's two chief works, *Discipleship* (published in 1937; the alternate English title is *The Cost of Discipleship*) and *Ethics* (mostly written 1939–1941, published posthumously). The earlier work is a classical exposition of the themes of radical discipleship: life in Christian community, living for others, crying out for the disadvantaged, and taking up the cross. Throughout, the inner clarity of the Sermon on the Mount, with Christ at the center, is paramount. Accordingly, love of enemies is a matter of simple faithfulness to the crucified Christ:

> Does [Jesus] refuse to face up to realities – or shall we say, to the sin of the world? . . . Jesus

tells us that it is just because we live in the world, and just because the world is evil, that the precept of nonresistance must be put into practice. Surely we do not wish to accuse Jesus of ignoring the reality and power of evil! Why, the whole of his life was one long conflict with the devil. He calls evil evil, and that is the very reason why he speaks to his followers in this way.[2]

The Bonhoeffer of *Ethics* is said to move away from this demand for simple obedience, concentrating instead on such notions as the human predicament of guilt, the duty to heed God's creational "mandates," and the distinction between "last things" and "things before the last." In this reading, *Ethics* represents a break with Bonhoeffer's earlier writings and opens up room to consider employing violent means in certain borderline situations. Killing might be one's Christian duty.

Does such a shift really occur in Bonhoeffer's thinking? The authors argue that it does not. At this point their argument becomes nuanced and assumes considerable familiarity with Bonhoeffer's oeuvre. They caution that the new approach in *Ethics* cannot be mistaken for an abandonment of earlier convictions. "Correction does not entail repudiation unless that which is correcting and that which is corrected are logically incompatible" (177). In a detailed analysis, they argue that Bonhoeffer's later writings actually expand the ethical project begun in *Discipleship*: "*Ethics* is its confirmation, as it is its continuation, amendment, clarification, and culmination" (158).

An example serves to illustrate the point. In *Discipleship,* there appears to be a marked opposition between the church on the one hand and the world on the other. The tone in *Ethics,* however, is quite different: God acts to reconcile the world to himself by becoming human;

---

2. Dietrich Bonhoeffer, *The Cost of Discipleship* (Touchstone, 1995), 143–144.

"Christianity without discipleship is always Christianity without Christ."

Dietrich Bonhoeffer

Jesus Christ is the redemption of the world and the restorer of communion. Christian faithfulness is made manifest, therefore, within the divine mandate of being responsible in and for the world.

Upon a closer look, however, this apparent contrast is just a matter of viewing the same thing from a different perspective. In *Discipleship* Bonhoeffer's focus is on the call of Christ and how this call forms the nature and mission of the church. *Ethics*, on the other hand, situates the church within a broader context of the whole world of God, of which the church forms a part. All the same, Christ remains just as much in the center as before. In the chapter "Ethics as Formation," for instance, Bonhoeffer holds up the person and action of Jesus Christ as exemplar, in direct opposition to ethical systems that reduce Christian ethics to a set of "Christian principles":

> What matters in the church is not religion but the form of Christ, and its taking form amidst a band of men. If we allow ourselves to lose sight of this, even for an instant, we inevitably relapse into that program-planning for the ethical or religious shaping of the world, which was where we set out from. . . . The only formation is formation by and into the form of Jesus

Christ. The point of departure for Christian ethics is the body of Christ, the form of Christ in the form of the church, and formation of the church in conformity with the form of Christ.[3]

Later in the book he drives the same point home:

> God's commandment is the only warrant for ethical discourse. . . . [Yet] the commandment of God is and always remains the commandment of God which is made manifest in Jesus Christ. There is no other commandment of God than that which is revealed by him and which is manifested according to his will in Jesus Christ.[4]

Only the form of Christ can shape Christian life; only through the person of Christ can we understand the world. This approach to Christian ethics, the authors observe, "is almost identical to that of *Discipleship*" (185). In both books, Bonhoeffer consistently criticizes any kind of ethic which is built on autonomous action. The call of the Christian is always a matter of obedience to Christ, who acts in and through his disciples living in the world.

This emphasis upon unconditional obedience to Christ comes vividly to the fore when Bonhoeffer – eschewing the traditional Reformation terminology of created "orders" or "estates" – refers to creational "mandates." Such mandates – family, work, education, government, religion – do not possess "a static, standalone character detached from ongoing divine authorization," let alone a separate ethic of their own in the manner of some Lutheran theology. On the contrary, all that matters is full obedience to Christ's command. Such obedience is not (contra Niebuhr) an "impossible possibility"; rather, through the church as the corporate form of Christ himself, God's redemptive love can meet and overcome evil

---

3. Dietrich Bonhoeffer, *Ethics* (Touchstone, 1995), 84.

4. Ibid., 277 – 279.

head-on. Christ is Lord over every sphere of existence: his command beckons us into public life, but always in a way that we are free to live for others *as Christ would* in the world.

The authors clarify that Bonhoeffer's pacifism had little to do with absolute moral principles. His commitment to nonresistance was rooted solely in the person of Christ: "God's commandments are true and valid because Christ is true and valid – an order that should not be reversed. When the commandments are, however, abstracted from their grounding in Christ's person and made into absolute moral principles, the person of Christ is made subservient to these moral standards" (185). In both *Discipleship* and *Ethics* Bonhoeffer rejects this possibility, insisting that Christ must always remain at the center.

Nation, Siegrist, and Umbel marshal an impressive case based on Bonhoeffer's life and thought. But there is weighty counterevidence to their thesis: recollections by some of Bonhoeffer's associates, notably Eberhard Bethge, that in the last years of his life Bonhoeffer had remarked that he was willing to kill Hitler, if necessary personally. (Even according to Bethge, Bonhoeffer's actual role in the conspiracy was marginal.) Here the authors make their boldest, and most controversial, move. They argue that memories after the fact cannot bear the evidentiary load of proving such a radical shift in Bonhoeffer's convictions – especially if they conflict with the otherwise united witness of the historical record and the trajectory of Bonhoeffer's thought. On this difficult point, the authors will not convince everyone, but they do shift the burden of proof. No longer is it possible to uncritically assume that Bonhoeffer discarded his pacifism in order to help plot the Führer's assassination.

Nor will it do, for that matter, to set up a simplistic opposition between pacifism – defined reductively as "not killing" – and a robust sense of responsibility to combat public wrong. To accept one does not require abandoning the other. As Bonhoeffer certainly realized, in situations of profound evil such as Nazi Germany all moral choices will be fraught with ambiguity and uncertain outcomes. For a Christian, the decision is not whether or not to keep one's hands clean (this is impossible anyway), but rather whether or not to walk obediently in the way of Jesus, trusting as he did in God's power.

What in the end are we to make of Bonhoeffer? His courage and sacrifice stand whether or not the authors are right; indeed some would call it futile, and impious, to flog the evidence in pursuit of certainty one way or the other. Yet for anyone who has ever doubted that this apostle of obedient discipleship would really violate a teaching of Jesus that he himself understood to be central, this book explains why such doubts may be justified. Well-crafted, judicious, and happily short on polemics, it is a work that should, in the words of Barry Harvey, "decisively reframe the way we read the thought and life of this most remarkable Christian."

For this reviewer, the book does much more. It recovers the Bonhoeffer who radically and consistently gave witness to the cross, a man to whom Jesus was all in all. As Bonhoeffer once put it: "The peace of Jesus is the cross. And this cross is the sword God wields on earth." Wielding this sword and no other, we are called to serve a crucified master – so Bonhoeffer teaches us – bringing peace in the way He brought peace, and conquering as He conquered. ➤

Charles E. Moore is co-editor of the Blumhardt Series from Plough Publishing and Cascade Books, which includes most recently the C.F. Blumhardt volume The Gospel of God's Reign: Living for the Kingdom of God *(2013).*

For One Bereaved

Stem and leaf and bud and flower,
growth perceptible each hour
to eyes slow enough to see.

Healing in the shattered bone
until each separate cell has grown
back to weight-bearing constancy.

The heart mends slowly, day by day,
not by man's wit, but in love's way,
rich-laden with the past, yet free.

Jane Tyson Clement

Digging Deeper *A Sermon on the Mount Reading List*

Scholarly treatments as well as popular books on the Sermon on the Mount abound. Although many are worthwhile (Dale Ellison's and Charles Quarles's come to mind), many more can be safely ignored. Here are six volumes that deserve special attention.

Must Reads: There is nothing quite like Eberhard Arnold's *Salt and Light.* In these selections from lectures and talks given in Germany between 1915 and 1935, Arnold calls decisively for a new, revolutionary way of discipleship. He speaks with a passion and longing that simply sweeps you off your feet. Each individual chapter addresses a particular feature of the Sermon on the Mount; taken collectively, the unrelenting clarity of Arnold's words propels one to action. He highlights again and again that Jesus' teaching is neither a new ethic nor a moral code but rather a proclamation: a witness to the reality of God's kingdom here on earth. Discipleship and community life belong together, and both belong to God's coming kingdom of complete love and justice.

Bonhoeffer's *The Cost of Discipleship* drives home Arnold's call to decisiveness by centering on the necessity of obeying Jesus' words. Bonhoeffer's rare ability to explain scripture in a way that is both illuminating and genuinely inspiring has made this perhaps the most influential book on the Sermon on the Mount for modern Christians. Writing under the nose of the Nazis, he develops his well-known emphasis on discipleship as a matter of "costly grace" – a call to make visible one's allegiance to Christ within a life of true Christian fellowship that encompasses every aspect of daily life.

Jumping forward to today, Scot McKnight's *Sermon on the Mount* (2013) does a marvelous job of drawing both practical and theological insights from Jesus' commands. McKnight is a New Testament scholar and so addresses many of the exegetical hot spots. Yet he does so in a way that is readily understandable and to the point, moving the reader easily from the text to lived experience. McKnight's tone is less passionate than Arnold's and Bonhoeffer's but no less bold: he is adamant that the Sermon on the Mount is potent as well as "supremely and irreducibly ecclesial" In addressing the many thorny interpretive questions, McKnight judiciously surveys the evidence and then offers his own take with thoughtfulness, grace, and brevity. Repeatedly he brings the reader back to the main issue: How can we obey Jesus' words today?

Recommended: John Stott's 1978 *Christian Counter-Culture* has become an evangelical classic. Relying on the metaphors of "salt and light" and focusing on Christian character, Stott beautifully highlights the radical nature of discipleship and the contrast between following Jesus and the conventional wisdom of this world. Stott is a teacher at heart and handles the text in a way that stimulates reflection.

From a more Anabaptist viewpoint, Glen Stassen's *Living the Sermon on the Mount* spells out the social implications of Jesus' teachings by asking how we are to pursue God's justice in the world. The outstanding feature of this volume is

Must Reads

Salt and Light
Living the Sermon
on the Mount
Eberhard Arnold
(Plough)

**The Cost
of Discipleship**
Dietrich Bonhoeffer
(Touchstone)

**Sermon
on the Mount**
Scot McKnight
(Zondervan)

Recommended

**Christian
Counter-Culture**
The Message of the
Sermon on the Mount
John Stott
(IVP)

**Living
the Sermon
on the Mount**
Glen H. Stassen
(Jossey-Bass)

**The Sermon
on the Mount
through the
Centuries**
*ed. Greenman,
Larsen, and Spencer*
(Brazos)

its emphasis on Jesus' transforming alternative to power, violence, injustice, and impurity.

Both Stott's and Stassen's books remind us that whenever we approach the Sermon on the Mount we do so historically and contextually. This is what makes *The Sermon on the Mount through the Centuries* so refreshing. A collection of essays by a dozen noteworthy writers including Robert Louis Wilken, Mark Noll, and Stanley Hauerwas, this volume enables the reader to appreciate the richness of Jesus' Sermon through the eyes of earlier believers including Chrysostom, Augustine, Luther, Wesley, Yoder, and Pope John Paul II. It's a refreshing read, and a humbling one. ➤

The Editors

BRIEFLY NOTED

My Poems Won't Change the World
Patrizia Cavalli, ed. Gini Alhadeff (FSG)

Few moments in the reading life give more pleasure than the unexpected discovery of a really good poet. This bilingual collection from Italian poet Patrizia Cavalli will give that opportunity to many fortunate readers. (See her poem page 30 of this issue.) You may find yourself enthusiastically repeating her lines to unsuspecting friends. The fact is, many of Cavalli's poems are irresistibly quotable – and funny and human and technically brilliant. Take this four-liner, for instance:

> Lame pigeon. Ridiculous
> lame crooked pigeon.
> When they have defects animals
> suddenly resemble humans.

The translations, by half a dozen poets including the editor, are generally excellent, which is to say that their inevitable failure to replicate the Italian in English comes off with warmth and grace.

Like Catullus, Cavalli is a master at playing the colloquial against the sublime, setting them up in a perilous counterpoise. She also shares the Latin poet's love for epigrams and for traditional forms, specifically the eleven-syllable line. Like Catullus again, many of her poems are anything but Christian; the same, of course, can be said about the works of Michelangelo. At its best, her poetry's intense, uncomplicated love of life and of the physical world yield a glimpse of an underlying reality – an "uncontainable splendor."

Jesus Was a Migrant
Deirdre Cornell (Orbis)

In this slim volume of reflections, Cornell weaves the biblical stories of exodus and exile, persecution and relocation with the realities of refugees and migrants today. "Migration has caused – and been caused by – tremendous suffering," she writes. "It has also served as a source of great blessing." Cornell is at her best telling stories of migrants whom she has befriended over the course of two decades of social work in U.S. trailer parks and remote Mexican villages. She mines her own Irish and Italian immigrant heritage and her roots in the Catholic Worker movement founded by Dorothy Day. While not all will feel at home with the book's deeply Catholic spirituality, we would all do well to be reminded of the biblical injunction to love our neighbor and welcome the stranger – and to remember that as Christians we are followers of a man who, like so many of our brothers and sisters today, had no place to lay his head. ➤

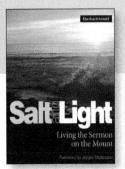

Current titles from Plough

Recommended Reading

Salt and Light: Living the Sermon on the Mount by Eberhard Arnold. A man who was ready to risk everything in his own quest to live out Jesus' self-sacrificing demands calls all of us to live for the Sermon's ultimate goal: building a just, peaceable society motivated by love. *"Simple, luminous, direct."* – Thomas Merton

God's Revolution: Justice, Community, and the Coming Kingdom by Eberhard Arnold. Christ's truths may heal and save, but to do so, they must first turn our lives upside down. Topical readings on church, state, community, and family tackle the root causes of suffering. *"Prophetic pastoral instruction."* – John Howard Yoder

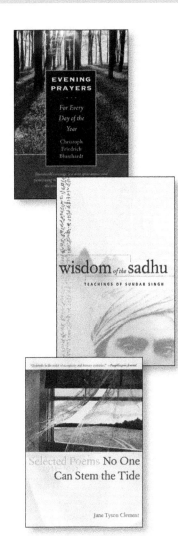

Evening Prayers: For Every Day of the Year by Christoph Friedrich Blumhardt. These daily prayers bespeak a certainty in God's nearness and a firm conviction that his kingdom is indeed on the way. This reassurance can bring even the most hectic day to a peaceful conclusion. *"A treasure, a precious pearl."* – Luci Shaw, author

Wisdom of the Sadhu: Teachings of Sundar Singh. An Indian mystic who embraced faith in Christ but eschewed Christianity's western trappings breathes fresh life into the gospel with his parables and meditations. *"Compelling . . . I highly recommend this book."* – Richard Foster

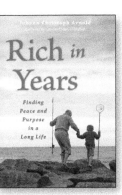

No One Can Stem the Tide: Selected Poems 1931–1991 by Jane Tyson Clement. In exploring the varied emotions of life – love and longing, struggle and frustration, joy and resolve – these poems reveal the tireless seeking of a generous and honest heart. *"Faith and radical optimism permeate these poems."* – St. Anthony's Messenger

Rich in Years: Finding Peace and Purpose in a Long Life by Johann Christoph Arnold. Why shouldn't old age be rewarding? A pastor whose books have helped over a million readers through life's challenges says our final years can be the richest season of our lives. *"Unassuming, yet outstanding. This is the best book I know on aging."* – J. I. Packer

Anni: Letters and Writings of Annemarie Wächter. A young woman coming of age in a time of cultural upheaval (1920s Germany) questions the meaning of life, faith, and friendship in this compelling true story told through her diary and letters. *"It is infinitely reassuring to know there is an absolute truth, an infinitely great love."* – from the book

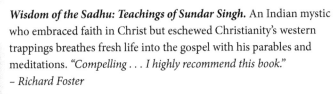
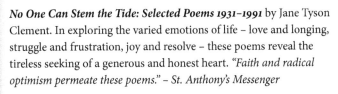

www.plough.com
*Free access to all e-books for **Plough Quarterly** subscribers.*

eric gill

& the story of Plough

It's 1937. Adolf Braun has taken refuge in England after being expelled from Hitler's Germany. Here he sets type for Plough's quarterly journal.

Of the many times that Plough Publishing House has moved its offices over the last century, the move in 1937 was the least planned. True, the publishing staff at the Rhön Bruderhof, a Christian community near Fulda, Germany, had known ever since Hitler's rise to power that time was running out. Still, it came as a surprise when on April 14, dozens of Gestapo and S.S. officers surrounded the property, confiscating all assets and imprisoning the board of directors. Those who remained were given forty-eight hours to leave the country.

By comparison, Plough's most recent move – last year, to new offices in Walden, New York – was calm and orderly. All the same, a few documents did get infuriatingly lost, while others unexpectedly came to light. One discovery was a dog-eared folder dated 1940 containing sketches for a Plough logo and letterhead design by a British typeface designer. His name was Eric Gill.

Even typography agnostics will recognize Gill's best-known typeface, Gill Sans – you have seen it in the BBC logo and on the jacket designs of Penguin Books. In my design-school years, I was so taken by its elegant precision that I made it the subject of a freelance research project. Although an intern at Plough at the time, I had no idea there was a connection.

Gill's logo design for Plough shows the simple silhouette of a mold-board plow, the kind that is pulled by horses and guided by

men. Its strong, clean lines are typical of Gill's work, as is the accuracy of form. When Gill drafted it, two years had already passed since the Bruderhof's suppression in Germany. In the meantime, the refugees had found a haven at the Ashton Keynes farm in the Cotswolds. Once they had established the utter basics – growing food, cooking, setting up child care – they set up a print shop and bindery and started publishing again.

Among their first projects was the first English-language edition of the community's periodical, *The Plough*. In Germany it had appeared in various formats since 1920, but now it became a quarterly journal carrying the tagline "Towards the Coming Order." By 1939, the magazine already counted Gill as a contributor.

A devoted Catholic, Gill was also a communitarian in his own right and deeply influenced by Tolstoy. Like G.K. Chesterton and Hilaire Belloc, he advocated Distributism, an economic model inspired by Catholic social teaching and its principles of solidarity and local community.

Among Gill's American admirers was fellow Distributist Peter Maurin, who co-founded the Catholic Worker Movement with Dorothy Day.

Gill, who was a sculptor and stonecutter as well as a designer, dreamed of escaping the "damned ugliness of all that capitalist industrialism produced," as he wrote in his autobiography. He believed that people should work with their hands and live together in such a way that work, art, faith, and daily life form an integrated whole:

> Neighborliness need not mean only loving-kindness and readiness to lend a hammer; it might also mean unanimity, an agreement in the mind as to the good and the true and the beautiful and a common practice founded thereon.

Accordingly, in 1913 Gill had founded a community of artists and craftsmen in the Sussex town of Ditchling, which one resident described as "a fascinating sort of communal early Christianity."[1]

The commonality with Plough's early Christian vision was obvious, which explains Gill's support for the magazine. I searched through several archival boxes looking for more details on the relationship, but found no further information.

As it turned out, Gill's logo design was never used, and remained undiscovered until now. Shortly after he submitted it in February 1940, the escalation of World War II forced Plough to close its English offices; almost all Bruderhof members emigrated to Paraguay in order to avoid the internment of German nationals. Gill's drawings were packed into a shipping crate, surviving the U-boats on its way to South America only to be forgotten amidst the challenges of pioneering in the jungle.

Sadly, the Plough logo would be among Gill's last designs. The rest of that year he spent

writing his autobiography. On November 17, 1940 he died.

Recent biographers have uncovered the moral disasters of Gill's personal life, which were previously unknown. Even so, he is remembered today as an innovative artist, a social visionary, and a man who, despite his failings, still strove to express his love for God through his work. In a letter to a friend he wrote:

> You cannot certainly paint a good picture by going to art school and learning a method, but must fall in love with God first and last. . . . So you cannot certainly walk with God by following a method, but must wait upon Him as a lover – singing beneath his window – waiting for him in the snow.[2]

Few artists have said it better. ⟶

Matina Horning

1 Fiona McCarthy, *Eric Gill* (Faber & Faber, 2011), 182. At least one Ditchling resident – Mari Marsden – would eventually join the Bruderhof; she is the mother of contributing artist Hannah Marsden (see page 52).

2 Eric Gill, *The Letters of Eric Gill,* ed. Walter Shewring (London: Jonathan Cape, 1947), 154.

Eric Gill's designs for Plough, 1940

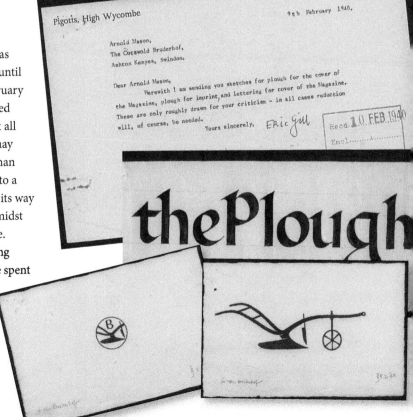

Katharina Hutter

Heroine of the Radical Reformation

JASON LANDSEL

On a summer evening in 1532 in the mountains of the South Tyrol, Anabaptist missionary Jakob Hutter baptized a young servant woman, Katharina Purst. She thus became one of thousands who were joining the Radical Reformation movement which had begun five years earlier in Switzerland. Dubbed "re-baptizers" or Anabaptists because of their practice of baptizing adults as a sign of voluntary discipleship, they quickly became the target of fierce persecution by both Catholic and Protestant rulers. (Thousands would be martyred over the next two decades.) Katharina was soon participating in the Anabaptist underground, bringing food and supplies to fellow believers hiding in the forests and remote mountain huts.

Three years later, in May 1935, Katharina married Jakob, who was now the leader of a growing community. Shortly afterward, the authorities evicted a large group of them from their homes, and the newlyweds led the refugees in a trek across the countryside. (This is the scene shown in my artwork opposite.) According to a contemporary account: "They were driven into the field like a herd of sheep. Nowhere were they permitted to camp until they reached [an outlying village]. . . . There they lay down on the wide heath under the open sky with many wretched widows and children, sick and infants."

Jakob begged their case to the local governor:

> Now we are camping on the heath. . . . We do not want to wrong or harm any human being, not even our worst enemy. Our walk in life is to live in truth and righteousness of God, in peace and unity. We do not hesitate to give an account of our conduct to anyone. But whoever says that we have camped on a field with so many thousands, as if we wanted war or the like, talks like a liar and a rascal. If all the world were like us there would be no war and no injustice. We can go nowhere; may God in heaven show us where we shall go.

The response to Jakob's letters was an intensified manhunt for him and Katharina. The couple spent the next four months moving from one safe house to the next, baptizing, encouraging demoralized believers, distributing donations to widows and the needy, and arranging for those in danger to flee to safety. Katharina seems to have built up a network of women who provided her and Jakob with shelter and assistance.

But in November, the two were arrested by officers of the bishop of Brixen, betrayed by an informer. Katharina was immediately separated from Jakob; so ended their married life together

Jason Landsel, *Forerunners: Katharina Hutter*
The artist writes: "This portrait of Katharina Hutter shows her as she leads a group of Anabaptist families fleeing from persecuting government forces. The scene is viewed through the eyes of the child she is leading. Both are in contemporary garb as a reminder that Katharina is not a figure of distant history but rather lives on as a sister in the faith."

The Forerunners art series will continue in future issues of *Plough Quarterly,* featuring courageous men and women of faith through the ages.

five months after it began. Katharina was still in prison in February when she would have heard that her husband, who had endured horrific tortures, had been burned at the stake in Innsbruck.[1] According to one source, she was expecting a baby.

Perhaps because her pregnancy resulted in relaxed security, in April Katharina managed to escape from prison; for the next two years she disappears from the historical record. In 1538 she was recaptured in her old mission ground. This time she was executed immediately, probably by drowning. She was around thirty years old.

Her last words have not come down to us, but letters from Jakob survive in which he fittingly sums up his and Katharina's shared calling: "I hope that God's fire will be so brightly kindled and his work so well established that even great floods and torrents of rain will not be able to quench the fire!" ⇒

---

1. In 2008, the Catholic bishops of Innsbruck and Bozen-Brixen wrote to Anabaptist communities expressing "deep regret" for their predecessors' role in the persecution.

Sources: *Chronicle of the Hutterian Brethren,* vol. 1, ed. Hutterian Brethren (Plough, 1987). *Quellen zur Geschichte der Täufer,* 14: *Osterreich III. Teil,* ed. Grete Mecenseffy (Gütersloh, 1983). C. Arnold Snyder and Linda A. Huebert Hecht, *Profiles of Anabaptist Women: Sixteenth-Century Reforming Pioneers* (Wilfrid Laurier UP, 2010).